ed
advancing

Student Book and CD-ROM

90

Course Companion
360Science

GCSE Additional Science

Foundation and Higher Tier

Pauline Anderson   Alan Philpotts

David Horrocks   Ian Roberts

Sue Jenkin   Richard Shewry

A PEARSON COMPANY

Edexcel
190 High Holborn
London WC1V 7BH
UK

ISBN 978-1-84690-160-7

Printed and bound in Great Britain by Scotprint, Haddington
Prepared for Edexcel by Starfish Design, Editorial and Project Management Ltd
Project management by Heather Morris
Illustrated by Peters and Zabransky (UK) Ltd
We are grateful to Oxford Designers and Illustrators Ltd for permission to reproduce
the illustrations on pp 9, 14, 16, 17, 25, 26, 35, 46, 47, 51, 53, 55, 58, 65, 67, 74,
79, 81 and 83.

The publisher's policy is to use paper manufactured from sustainable forests.

Contents

This new course will help you to understand the science around you that affects everyday life, and to develop your own practical scientific skills and knowledge. It includes Biology, Chemistry and Physics; each science has four interesting and useful topics that also form part of the separate GCSE Biology, GCSE Chemistry and GCSE Physics qualifications.

Biology Topic 1 Inside living cells

In this topic you will look at the role of DNA in your cells; how it controls the manufacture of protein and how respiration produces the necessary energy. You will also consider some uses of DNA technology.
- What is the structure of DNA and where is it found in your cells?
- What part do DNA and RNA play in the creation of proteins from amino acids?
- Where do your cells get energy from?
- What does respiration really mean?
- Why do you sometimes get cramp when you do a lot of exercise?
- What has this got to do with a healthy lifestyle?
- Why do some people think that fermenters can improve the quality of life?

Biology Topic 2 Divide and develop

This topic is all about how animal and plant cells grow and replicate.
- Growing makes your body get bigger, but do the cells get bigger or do you make more cells?
- How are your sex cells different from ordinary cells?
- Why is there such a controversy in the media about stem cells and research?
- What happens to your cells if you get cancer?
- How can we make plants produce more fruit and grow more?
- How did scientists produce Dolly the sheep?
- Why are many people worried about gene therapy and genetic modification?

Biology Topic 3 Energy flow

This topic is about sustainable food production across the world. You will discuss some of the effects that humans have already caused.
- How does photosynthesis really work and why is it so important?
- How was global warming caused and what can we do about it?
- How are 'factory farming', fertilisers and green algae on streams linked?
- How do plants get the minerals they need, such as nitrogen?
- Is it ethical that people in many countries don't get enough to eat, yet people in Britain are getting fatter?
- How do the carbon and nitrogen cycles help to maintain our biosphere?
- Could there ever be a biosphere on Mars?

Biology Topic 4 Interdependence

In this topic you will discuss the impact of human activity on the world's resources. You will be able to explore the ideas of conservation and biodiversity.
- Why does killing all the fish in a river have such a bad effect on the rest of the wildlife?
- How does the way you live affect the environment?
- Can we measure what effect people have had on their environment?
- Is it important to protect the natural environment and populations of wildlife?
- Does recycling really work?
- How does conservation management help biodiversity?

Chemistry Topic 5 Synthesis

This topic provides an introduction to the exciting world of organic chemistry. It also introduces chemical calculations and deals with some of the issues industrial scientists have to consider when making new materials.
- Have you heard of methane, ethane, propane and butane? Their names have similar endings, but what else do they have in common?
- Find out about the differences in reactivity between the alkanes and the alkenes.
- Have you heard the term 'polyunsaturated'? What does it mean?
- Did you know that polymers are made from monomers by very simple reactions?
- There are many different types of plastics, yet did you know that they are all made from the same starting material?
- You will learn how to use chemical equations to calculate masses of reactants and products in chemical reactions.
- You can find out about the term 'atom economy' and why it is important to scientists.

Chemistry Topic 6 In your element

This topic develops ideas on the periodic table introduced in GCSE Science, and shows how useful the periodic table is to chemists. You will learn about the tiny particles which make up atoms, and how such knowledge can explain crystal structure, electrolysis, isotopes, and chemical reactivity.
- Have you heard the words 'proton', 'neutron' and 'electron' before? What is the difference between them?
- Have you ever looked at a grain of salt with a hand lens and wondered about the flat surfaces and sharp edges?
- Have you ever passed an electric current through sea water and wondered how it is that two different gases are produced?
- Are all isotopes dangerous?
- Why is it that some elements are very reactive and others totally unreactive?

- Why is it that on the periodic table, most elements have their atomic masses quoted to several decimal places?
- How can trends in chemical reactivity be explained by electronic configurations?

Chemistry Topic 7 Chemical structures

This topic also develops the periodic table, concentrating on the electronic structures of atoms, and why this is relevant to the formation of covalent bonding. You will learn why these issues are important when considering the properties of compounds with different structures.

- Have you heard of buckminster fullerene or nanotubes?
- Does homeopathic medicine work? Do scientists find the ideas difficult to accept?
- How do metals conduct electricity?
- How can diamond and graphite possibly be made of the same atoms?
- How can dot and cross diagrams represent simple molecular structures?
- What is meant by the term 'giant structure'?
- How can simulation software be used in three-dimensional modelling?

Chemistry Topic 8 How fast? How furious?

There is the opportunity for lots of practical work in this unit! You will learn about the different factors that can affect the rate of a reaction and how you can detect the heat changes when chemical reactions take place. Finally, there is the opportunity to consider reactions which do not go to completion, ending up instead as a dynamic equilibrium!

- Have you heard the terms exothermic and endothermic?
- Did you know that reactions only take place when particles collide?
- What are the factors that affect the rate of chemical reactions?
- Why is the speeding up of reactions important to the maintenance of life?
- What is a reversible reaction and how can you change the equilibrium position?
- Why do farmers use artificial fertiliser?
- What is the Haber process and why is it important?

Physics Topic 9 As fast as you can

During this topic you will explore how forces can change your speed and direction or twist you round as you move. Theme park rides do these in a thrilling but safe way.

- What forces act on you when you jump out of an aeroplane and what do they do to you?
- How does a parachute help and what is different in a bungee jump?

- Are theme park rides made as exciting as possible or limited for safety?
- Has research into the design of Formula 1 cars made ordinary cars safer?
- You could be killed as you cross the road. So, why do it?

Physics Topic 10 Roller coasters and relativity

What are the similarities between the Moon orbiting the Earth, a roller coaster descending a steep slope and an electron going round a nucleus? All this and some thoughts about Einstein too! A possibility for extra study could be a trip to a theme park.

- What energy changes take place as a roller coaster goes round one circuit?
- Why do I not fall out of a roller coaster when I loop the loop?
- Do all theme park rides use forces in the same way?
- Einstein was not an experimental scientist, but did he do more than just think, like the ancient Greeks?

Physics Topic 11 Putting radiation to use

Radioactivity can kill but is not dangerous if treated carefully. Early researchers died from its effects but nowadays there are a wide variety of uses.

- If the radiations are so dangerous, how can they be used in medicine?
- What safety precautions will keep us safe?
- How can we measure time using a radioactive clock?
- The Earth is about 4500 million years old and there are still radioactive materials on it. How long does it take to become safe – is two half-lives enough?
- What are cosmic rays?

Physics Topic 12 Power of the atom

How can something smaller than an atom be responsible for creating things we can see millions of millions of miles away? This topic covers atoms and stars, as well as such down to Earth things as preventing electric shocks.

- What is needed for a nuclear explosion?
- How is a chain reaction controlled to give the steady supply of energy needed in a power station?
- Are nuclear reactors a development of our high-tech, modern technology or have they occurred in nature?
- Why can't you make a star in a test tube?
- When do we not want sparks, or how does a photocopier work?

How Science Works

How science works is a part of all the science you study. It is both about understanding the science you meet in everyday life and about how you carry out your own scientific investigations. In studying the twelve topics in GCSE Additional Science your teacher will help you to develop knowledge and understanding of how science works in that context. Understanding how science works will help you to:

- develop practical skills
- identify the questions that science can and cannot answer
- understand how scientists look for the answers
- evaluate scientific claims by judging the reliability and validity of the evidence
- question scientific reports in the media
- communicate your own findings clearly
- consider scientific findings in a wider context – recognising the difference between a fact and a theory
- make informed judgements about science and technology, including any ethical issues that may arise.

There are four aspects to developing your understanding of how science works:

1 Practical and enquiry skills

Scientists have to plan investigations and experiments to find evidence to support their ideas or put forward an answer to a scientific problem. They might want to:

- test a scientific idea
- answer a scientific question
- solve a scientific problem.

The important part of designing practical experiments is to ensure that the tests are fair, that reliable data are collected and the investigation is safe.

2 Data, evidence, theories and explanations

Scientists collect and analyse data. This might be primary data from their own experiments or secondary data from someone else's, often reported on the internet. If the data is secondary, they must be very careful to say where the data came from, by giving the name of the website, etc. Scientists will always look at their data and how they collected them to make sure they are safe and accurate.

- Was the method used the right one?
- Are the data accurate enough?
- Are the data valid and reliable so that they can be used as evidence?

If scientists are confident about their data, these could then be used to develop an argument to say what the evidence shows, and would be used to draw a conclusion. It is very important that any conclusion is well supported by the evidence.

Many people follow the latest fashion in diets, and most find they cannot stick to the diet. They often do not look to see if there is scientific evidence to support whether the diet works, or what the side effects might be.

Scientists use data from experiments and models to create theories that explain events or phenomena. Scientific theories are not just guesswork but are based on reliable evidence.

3 Communication skills

Scientists communicate with each other to share ideas and to see how others feel about their ideas. They communicate with the general public so that everyone knows what they have found out and how those ideas might be used.

Scientific ideas and information need to be analysed, interpreted and questioned. This is how scientists look at each other's work. If another scientist cannot carry out the experiment someone has tried and get the same results, the scientist would be very suspicious. In 2006, a South Korean scientist's work on stem cells was shown to be based on false data.

Data and information need to be converted into a form that other people can understand. Scientists often use ICT tools such as spreadsheets to help them do this. Spreadsheet data can be converted into graphs which are often easier to understand. Graphs could then be used in a slide presentation to communicate to other people. Scientists use ICT equipment to get better precision in their results. A digital thermometer is more precise than an alcohol thermometer.

4 Applications and implications of science

Many scientific and technological advances have benefits, drawbacks and risks. Often decisions about science and technology are difficult, because they raise ethical issues, and these decisions may have social, economic and environmental consequences. For example, science can give accurate information about the viability of a foetus at each stage of its development. That is why, in British law, a foetus can be terminated up to 24 weeks of its development. Science is not able to answer the ethical questions about whether it is right to terminate a foetus, or whether stem cells from human embryos should be used in research (see p.18).

What will I need to gain a good GCSE Additional Science grade?

At the end of the course – what qualification will I achieve?

You are working towards gaining a GCSE Additional Science qualification and during the course there will be opportunities to find out how well you understand how science works. Your teacher will ask you questions in class or homework that will help you to assess whether you understand and know the science in the twelve topics. In addition to the day-to-day help from your teacher in assessing your progress, you will be required to take assessments set by Edexcel. It will be Edexcel that will award your final grade for GCSE Additional Science.

This course is assessed in three ways.

Assessment of practical skills (10% of total marks)

Your teacher will assess three skills:

- how well you follow instructions (probably given on a worksheet)
- how good you are at collecting data safely, accurately and reliably
- your ability to present results in tables with headings and units.

Your teacher may gave you further guidance on when and where they will be watching you carry out some work in the laboratory. There are more details on the CD to explain what your teacher will be looking for in the observation. The main aim for you is to try to improve your practical skills during the course so that you achieve the highest mark possible in the three skill areas.

Assessment activities (30% of total marks)

These activities are set by Edexcel. Your teacher will decide when you will take one of these assessments during the course. There is an assessment activity for each of the twelve topics in GCSE Additional Science. The ones you are asked to take on completing a topic will depend on the plan for your course. In some instances you may take more than one in Biology, Chemistry or Physics. You have to do one of each subject. The highest score from each subject will account for 10% of your total score – making a possible 30% in total.

How will I be assessed for the remaining 60% of marks?

In consultation with your teachers, you should enter **two** of these three assessment units for each of Biology, Chemistry and Physics. You will do six assessments in total each worth 10%. Two of the options are written papers, and one is set and marked by your teachers. Your teacher will discuss with you whether to enter the Foundation or the Higher tier.

The text in this book in green is for Higher Tier students only.

For Biology, you will do **two** from these **three** assessment units.

1. A 20-minute multiple choice test (at either Higher or Foundation tier) covering all the Biology topics in the course.
2. A 30-minute tiered (i.e. Foundation or Higher tier) paper covering all of the Biology topics. This will be entirely made up of structured questions.
3. A task based on the Biology topics. This will be set and marked by your teachers. It may require you to produce a booklet, a presentation, a poster, a survey, etc. Your teacher will decide which type of activity is the best for you to do.

For Chemistry, you will do **two** from these **three** assessment units.

1. A 20-minute multiple choice test (at either Higher or Foundation tier) covering all the Chemistry topics in the course.
2. A 30-minute tiered (i.e. Foundation or Higher tier) paper covering all of the Chemistry topics (as for Biology).
3. A task based on the Chemistry topics. This will be set and marked by your teachers (as for Biology).

For Physics, you will do **two** from these **three** assessment units.

1. A 20-minute multiple choice test (at either Higher or Foundation tier) covering all the Physics topics in the course.
2. A 30-minute tiered (i.e. Foundation or Higher tier) paper covering all of the Physics topics (as for Biology).
3. A task based on the Physics topics. This will be set and marked by your teachers (as for Biology).

And finally

Your final GCSE Additional Science grade will be awarded by Edexcel based on your total score from:

practical skills – out of 10%
assessment activities – out of 30%
assessment units for Biology, Chemistry and Physics – out of 60%

This makes a total out of 100%. Throughout the course your teacher will have discussed with you a target grade. Your challenge is to take the opportunity to meet your target and achieve the highest grade possible.

Examiner's tips on how to achieve your target grade

Science lessons

Before a science lesson
- Glance through your notes.
- Write down three SMART targets for success.
- Check that you have your pen, pencil, calculator and books.

What are SMART targets?
Small
Measurable
Achievable
Realistic
Time limited
'I will learn 15 vocabulary words on 'Energy Flow' on Monday' is better than 'I will do some Biology revision next week'.

During the lesson
- Stay on task.
- Make your notes clear.
- Ask sensible questions.

After the lesson
- Make a short summary of the lesson.
- Write down questions to ask in your next lesson.
- Practise questions from the book.

Preparing for assessment activities and tests

Make summaries of your notes in your own words.

Review and grade your notes.
1. I can do and I know this.
2. I understand this but I don't know this yet.
3. I don't understand this and I don't know this yet.

Ask for help with the work you don't understand.

Learn: your vocabulary, equations, how things work, labels on diagrams, units

Make memory aids for yourself if you find these helpful. For example, the difference between meiosis and mitosis can be remembered with '**M**aking **E**ggs **I**n **O**varies, **S**perm **I**n **S**emen'.

When you have finished a topic practise exam questions on that topic – look on the CD for some examples.

Practise questions
- Write specimen answers and check them against the mark scheme.
- If you get it wrong try again after some more revision.
- Pretend you are the examiner and write a mark scheme for the question.

The day before a test
- Check your pens etc work and are in your bag.
- Get enough sleep.
- Don't cram, just read through your summaries.

Taking the test
- Check how long the test is and work out where you need to be by the half-way stage.
- Read the instructions and the introduction to each question carefully.
- Look at how many marks are given for each part of each question.
- Make a point for each mark.
- If you get stuck, move on to the next question but remember to come back to it if you have time.
- Write in the space provided or use extra sheets.
- Make your writing legible and in dark blue or black pen – the examiner has to be able to read it if he is to mark it.
- Use the correct vocabulary.
- Read through your work carefully and critically at the end.

Doing calculations
- Write down the equation.
- Make it clear what values you are substituting.
- Write down your working out.
- Set out your working neatly.
- Remember to add the units.

Inside living cells

1 DNA

Have you ever wondered?

How does my body know which enzymes to produce?

Key facts

- Genes are made of a chemical called DNA.
- DNA contains the genetic code for making proteins.
- Enzymes are a type of protein that control all chemical reactions in cells.
- A molecule of DNA is made up from sugars, phosphates and bases.
- The bases are in sequences of three called a triplet. Each triplet codes for one amino acid.
- Proteins are made from long chains of amino acids.
- There are about 20 different amino acids.
- Every protein has amino acids in a different order. This order controls the structure and function of the protein.

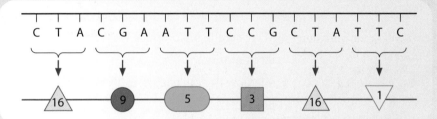

The order of base triplets in the DNA coding strand produces the order of the amino acids in the protein.

❶ Examiner's tips

- You should know the structure of DNA and about the base pairs.
- You should know about the shape of the DNA molecule and how this enables it to do its job.
- You need to know how the genetic code results in the formation of chains of amino acids.
- You need to know how the amino acid chains result in different proteins being made.

Can you answer these questions?

1. What are the four bases in the DNA molecule?
2. How do the bases line up in the DNA molecule?
3. How does a triplet code for a particular amino acid?
4. How are enzymes made?

Definitions

- **amino acid** One of about 20 different small molecules that link together in long chains to form proteins. Often called the building blocks of proteins.
- **bases** Chemical groups making up part of the DNA and RNA molecules. The order of the bases in the DNA forms the genetic code.
- **DNA** The chemical that makes up genes (deoxyribonucleic acid).
- **triplet** A group of three bases in DNA that codes for the placing of an amino acid in a protein during protein synthesis.

Look on the CD for more exam practice questions

Did you know?

- In 1953 Francis Crick calmly announced that 'we have found the secret of life'. With James Watson he had discovered the double helix structure of DNA.

② Fermentation and microorganisms

Key facts

- Microorganisms are tiny living things that can be seen using a microscope and include bacteria, yeasts and moulds.
- Microorganisms can be cultivated in a culture medium.
- Microorganisms produce waste products and other substances by **fermentation**.
- Microorganisms can be **cultivated** in a fermenter to make many different products.
- Scientists can genetically modify microorganisms so that they make useful products.
- Microorganisms have been used for thousand of years to make food like bread, cheese and soy sauce.
- A fermenter is kept at optimum conditions so the microorganisms can produce maximum yield.
- A fermenter is kept under aseptic conditions to avoid contamination of the product.

❶ Examiner's tips

- You should know about the process of culturing microorganisms in a fermenter.
- A bacterium can be genetically modified by inserting a section of DNA into it.
- Insulin and penicillin are two useful products made in a fermenter.
- Mycoprotein is used as a meat substitute.
- You should know why a fermenter is kept at optimum conditions and why aseptic conditions are important.

Definitions

- **cultivated**
  The growth of organisms, such as plants and microorganisms, in controlled conditions.
- **fermentation**
  Using microorganisms to break down nutrients into useful products.

Can you answer these questions?

1. What is a culture medium?
2. What is fermentation?
3. Explain how bacteria can be genetically modified to produce insulin
4. What are the advantages of using microorganisms for food production?

Look on the CD for more exam practice questions

Did you know?

- Yoghurt is made using microorganisms.

③ Proteins

Have you ever wondered?

Why are plants and animals so different?

Key facts

- **Protein** synthesis is the process of making proteins inside cells.
- The instructions for making proteins are carried by the DNA in the nucleus of the cell.
- The instructions are copied from the DNA and carried to the **ribosomes** by **RNA**.
- Proteins are assembled from amino acids by ribosomes.
- The order of the amino acids in the protein is controlled by the triplets of bases in the genetic code.
- Amino acids are joined together in the right sequence to form long chains called polypeptides.
- Polypeptide chains are folded into a particular shape to form the protein.

❶ Examiner's tips

- You need to know how the genetic code is copied from the DNA to make messenger RNA.
- You need to know how the code on the messenger RNA is translated by transfer RNA into a sequence that is used to join amino acids into a chain.
- You need to know that the chains of amino acids are folded into special shapes to create a unique shape for each different protein.

Definitions

- **protein** A chemical made of chains of amino acids. Proteins form part of the cell's framework (structural proteins) or carry out a particular job (functional proteins).
- **ribosome** A tiny organelle in the cytoplasm of a cell where proteins are made.
- **RNA** A chemical similar to DNA that is involved in protein synthesis.

Can you answer these questions?

1. What is the difference between DNA and RNA?
2. How is the genetic code carried by a DNA molecule?
3. Why are triplets of bases important?
4. How many types of RNA are there?

Look on the CD for more exam practice questions

Did you know?

- The human body can make many amino acids. There are eight it cannot make and these are an essential part of your diet. They are: leucine, isoleucine, valine, threonine, methionine, phenylalanine, tryptophan, lysine.

④ Respiration

Have you ever wondered?

What processes in cells keep you alive?

Key facts

- The body needs glucose, from which it releases energy.
- Glucose and oxygen react in the cells of your body to release energy.
- Carbon dioxide and water are produced as waste products.
- The process of releasing energy is called respiration.
- When oxygen is used the process is called **aerobic** respiration.
- Both oxygen and glucose pass into cells by **diffusion** from the blood.
- Carbon dioxide diffuses out of cells into the blood.
- Respiration increases with exercise to provide more energy.
- Vigorous exercise means that oxygen cannot be delivered fast enough to respiring cells.
- When there is insufficient oxygen, glucose is converted into lactic acid to release energy.
- Respiration without oxygen is called anaerobic respiration.
- A buildup of lactic acid can cause cramp.

Definitions

- **aerobic** A process using oxygen. Aerobic respiration is respiration that needs oxygen.
- **diffusion** The movement of molecules from a region where they are at a high concentration to a region where they are at a low concentration.

Look on the CD for more exam practice questions

Examiner's tips

- You should be able to write the word equation for respiration.
- You should understand how diffusion takes place from regions of high concentration to regions of low concentration, and how this works with respiring cells.
- You should be able to explain why respiration takes place inside cells.
- You should know the differences between aerobic and anaerobic respiration.

Can you answer these questions?

1. Why is respiration needed?
2. What is the difference between aerobic and anaerobic respiration?
3. Write the word equation for aerobic respiration.
4. What is meant by diffusion?
5. What causes cramp?

Did you know?

- You can get 2900 kJ of energy from one glucose molecule during aerobic respiration.

⑤ Exercise

Have you ever wondered?

Why do I get cramp?

Key facts

- Vigorous exercise means that muscles need more energy to do the extra work.
- Increased **respiration** provides more energy.
- Increased respiration requires more oxygen and glucose to be delivered to muscle cells.
- Increased respiration requires carbon dioxide to be removed from muscle cells.
- The breathing system must work harder to get more oxygen into the blood and to remove carbon dioxide from the blood.
- The heart rate increases to increase the flow of blood to the muscles.
- Breathing and heart rate can be measured in different ways to increase the reliability of the data.

	Time (minutes)	Kelly's results		Rutvi's results	
		Breathing rate (breaths/minute)	Heart rate (beats/minute)	Breathing rate (breaths/minute)	Heart rate (beats/minute)
Cycling	0	14	74	12	76
	5	19	122	16	99
	10	24	139	16	103
	15	27	145	16	103
Resting	20	13	90	12	75
	25	14	75	12	76

Table showing the effect of exercise on breathing and heart rate.

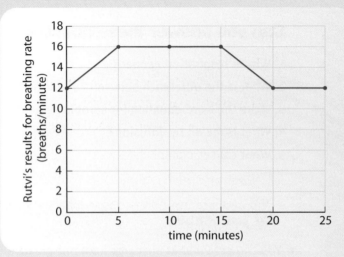

Graph showing breathing rate over the 25 minute period.

Definitions

- **respiration** The chemical reaction occurring in all living cells. Glucose is broken down into carbon dioxide and water to release energy.

Look on the CD for more exam practice questions

❶ Examiner's tips

- Increased heart rate increases the amount of blood pumped around the body.
- Increased breathing rate increases the amounts of oxygen taken in and carbon dioxide expelled.
- You need to be able to interpret data on heart rate and breathing rate, including describing patterns and trends shown in graphs.
- You should understand that measurements can be improved by using equipment that is more precise.

Can you answer these questions?

1. Why does heart rate increase during vigorous exercise?
2. Describe the shape of the graph of Rutvi's results, and explain why this changes.
3. How does increased breathing rate help to increase energy release during exercise?
4. Why is a digital thermometer more precise then an alcohol thermometer?

Did you know?

- You breathe about 0.5 litres in a normal breath, but have a capacity to breathe 4 to 6 litres of air.

⑥ Diet and exercise

Key facts

- A healthy **diet** and regular exercise are important for good health.
- A lot of research is needed to find out what a good diet is.
- Research shows that high **cholesterol** foods can affect your health, particularly your heart.
- There are many other factors which affect heart disease.
- Some research now shows that cholesterol-containing foods may not be so dangerous if used in moderation.
- People follow fashionable diets even though there is little evidence that the diets work.
- An excess of any kind of food can be unhealthy.
- A well balanced diet containing lots of fresh fruit and vegetables with regular exercise is needed for good health.

Definitions

- **cholesterol** A fatty deposit that can build up and block arteries.
- **diet** Eating a wide variety of different foods to gain all the nutrients we need.

Look on the CD for more exam practice questions

❶ Examiner's tips

- The evidence behind the claims for a diet or exercise regime needs careful consideration.
- Popular opinion is easily influenced by claims and scare stories that have no scientific evidence to back them up.
- You should know the basic components of a healthy diet.

Can you answer these questions?

1. Why do many people believe that too much cholesterol in your food is dangerous?
2. Suggest reasons why it may be dangerous to follow the latest diet fashion.
3. What is meant by 'a healthy lifestyle'?
4. Why is regular exercise important?

Did you know?

- One in five people are so overweight they are classed as obese. About four in every hundred people suffer from anorexia and are dangerously underweight.

Divide and develop

1 Cell division

Key facts
- New cells are made by cell division.
- Body cells are made by a process called mitosis, producing cells for growth, repair, or the replacement of older cells.

Mitosis is the division of a cell to produce two identical new cells.

Each chromosome makes an identical copy of itself

The chromosomes line up across the centre of the cell.

One complete set of chromosomes moves to each end of the cell.

The cell starts to divide in two and split apart. Each new cell is a daughter cell. The daughter cells contain identical chromosomes in their nuclei and carry identical genes to the parent cell.

- A cell makes a copy of its **chromosomes** before it divides.
- After a cell divides, each new cell contains identical chromosomes with identical genes.
- Meiosis is cell division to produce **gametes**.
- Meiosis halves the number of chromosomes when gametes are formed.
- Both mitosis and meiosis start with diploid cells: mitosis produces **diploid** cells but meiosis produces **haploid** cells.

Definitions
- **chromosomes** Long DNA molecules in the nucleus that carry genetic information.
- **gametes** Sex cells, such as sperm, ova and pollen.
- **diploid** A cell that contains the full set of 46 chromosomes.
- **haploid** A cell that contains 23 (half) the full number of chromosomes. Produced by meiosis.

❶ Examiner's tips
- You should know the sequence of events in mitosis.
- Plants can keep on growing all their lives, but most animals stop growing when they reach a certain size.
- You should know the sequence of events in meiosis.
- You need to know the differences between mitosis and meiosis.

Look on the CD for more exam practice questions

Can you answer these questions?

1. How does mitosis produce identical cells?
2. Why is cell division needed?
3. How does meiosis produce gametes?
4. What are the differences between mitosis and meiosis?

Did you know?

- The tallest plant in the world is a Giant Redwood, 115 m high and still growing!

② Growth

Have you ever wondered?

Why don't I keep growing forever?

Key facts

- Growth is a permanent increase in the size or mass of an organism.
- There are several different ways to measuring growth.
- When cells divide they may undergo **differentiation** and develop special characteristics so that they can do their job.
- Plant cells grow by dividing then absorbing water into their vacuoles.
- Humans start life as a fertilised cell called a zygote, which develops into a **foetus**.
- Humans grow at a steady rate from after the first year until the growth spurt at puberty.
- Height is a continuous variable and follows a normal distribution curve.

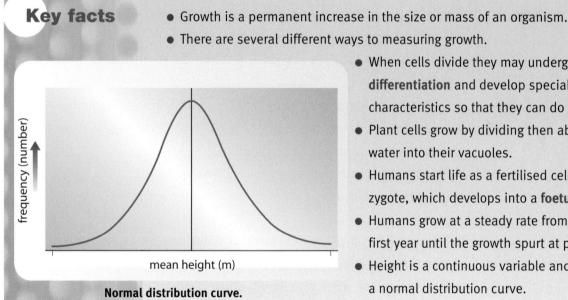

Normal distribution curve.

Definitions

- **differentiation** In cells, the process whereby new cells develop special characteristics to allow them to do their job.
- **foetus** The name for an embryo after the eighth week of development in the womb.

❶ Examiner's tips

- Know the different ways of measuring growth in plants and other organisms.
- Know the factors that can affect the way plants grow.
- Know that a zygote develops into an embryo and then into a foetus.
- Explain why girls have a growth spurt at a younger age than boys.
- Understand what a normal distribution is and use human height as an example.

Look on the CD for more exam practice questions

Can you answer these questions?

1. What is meant by growth?
2. Why do some dividing cells undergo differentiation?
3. What factors can affect the way plants grow?
4. How does size change during human growth?

Did you know?

- A human foetus increases its mass around 3000 times in the final 30 weeks of pregnancy.

③ Stem cells, tough decisions

Have you ever wondered?

What is a stem cell and why do scientists think it is so valuable?

Key facts

- Cells do not live forever but lose the ability to divide. The maximum number of cell divisions is called the Hayflick limit.
- Cancer cells do not have a Hayflick limit and can keep dividing to form a tumour.
- **Stem cells** can develop into any kind of cell. They are undifferentiated.
- Scientists are very excited about the possibility that stem cells could be used to treat many medical conditions.
- The most useful stem cells come from human embryos.
- Many people think that it is wrong to use human embryos for medical research.
- Science tells us that a human foetus is viable from 24 weeks, but **termination** is an ethical issue.
- Athletes can use steroids to improve their performance, but many people have ethical concerns about this.

Definitions

- **stem cell** A cell that has the ability to become any type of cell in an organism.
- **termination** Deliberately ending a pregnancy.

❶ Examiner's tips

- You need to know why stem cells have so much potential.
- You should understand why embryo stem cells have more potential than stem cells from adults.
- Think about the ethical issues behind using embryos for medical research, and why termination is such a difficult issue.
- Think about why sports people take steroids to enhance their performance, and why there are medical and ethical concerns about this.

Look on the CD for more exam practice questions

Can you answer these questions?

1. Explain why a cancer cell is dangerous.
2. Explain why a stem cell has no Hayflick limit.
3. Why are so many people against stem cell research?
4. Why is a 36 week old foetus viable when a 16 week old one is not?
5. What side effects can taking steroids have on athletes?

Did you know?

- Termination of a pregnancy is legal up to the 24th week in the UK.

4 Plant growth

Have you ever wondered?

Why do plants need hormones?

Key facts

- Plants need certain conditions to grow.
- Plants need light for photosynthesis. This process is the source of all the chemicals plants need for growth.
- Plants need mineral salts from the soil to provide **nutrients**.
- Temperature affects plant processes like photosynthesis. Many plants have adaptations to help them cope with extremes of temperature.
- Plant **hormones** control growth, flowering and fruit ripening.
- Auxin is a plant hormone which controls the growth of stems towards light and roots downwards.
- Artificial hormones can be used by fruit growers to make fruit develop or ripen.

Definitions

- **hormones** Chemicals produced by a living organism which regulate growth, metabolism, and other important processes.
- **nutrient** One of the chemicals needed by an organism to grow.

❶ Examiner's tips

- Plants are adapted to certain conditions in which they grow best. Some plants can survive extreme conditions that would be hostile to other plants.
- Plants have hormones that control how they grow.
- You should know how auxin controls the growth of shoots and roots.

Can you answer these questions?

1. Name conditions that affect plant growth.
2. Explain why plants need light and how some plants can grow in low light conditions where others can not.
3. Explain how auxin controls the growth of a shoot towards light.
4. Explain how hormones cause fruit to develop.

Look on the CD for more exam practice questions

Did you know?

- The tree-line is the limit beyond which conditions are too hostile for trees to grow.

⑤ Artificial selection and cloning

Have you ever wondered?

Why do scientists want to modify cows?

Key facts

- Some **species** can replace body parts. This is called regeneration.
- Stem cell research might lead to regeneration of human body parts.
- Selective breeding has been going on for thousands of years.
- Selective breeding means breeding from individuals that have the characteristics you want, and then repeating the process with their offspring.
- Selective breeding is used to improve the quality and quantity of crops and domesticated animals.
- A clone is a genetic copy of another single organism.
- The commonest form of cloning is cell nuclear transfer.
- **Genetic modification** involves introducing genes into the DNA of an organism to change its genetic characteristics.
- There are ethical issues concerning cloning and genetic modification.

Definitions

- **genetic modification** Changing the genetic characteristics of an organism by manipulating genes and introducing them into its DNA.
- **species** A group of living things sharing the same characteristics which breed together to produce young.

❶ Examiner's tips

- You need to be able to explain the process of selective breeding.
- You should be able to give some reasons why selective breeding is used.
- You need to be able to explain the steps in the process of cloning.
- You need to understand the arguments for and against cloning and genetic modification.

Can you answer these questions?

1. What is meant by regeneration?
2. How could dairy cows be selectively bred to give more milk?
3. Explain the process of cloning a genetically identical individual.
4. What are the arguments for and against cloning?

Look on the CD for more exam practice questions

Did you know?

- Norman Borlaug won the Nobel Prize for his work on the selective breeding of dwarf wheat to create new varieties with higher yield.

⑥ Gene therapy

Have you ever wondered?

How can gene therapy help cancer sufferers?

Key facts

- Many human diseases are caused by faulty genes. For example, **cancer cells** divide uncontrollably due to faulty genes.
- Cystic fibrosis and haemophilia are genetic diseases.
- Gene therapy means replacing a faulty gene with one that works properly.
- Gene therapy might stop diseases being passed from one generation to the next.
- The replacement gene is carried by a virus.
- There may be long term risks in using gene therapy.
- Gene therapy can to help treat sufferers from some forms of cancer.
- There are several gene therapy techniques being investigated that have the potential to treat other forms of cancer.

Definitions

- **cancer cell** A cell that divides uncontrollably due to faulty genes.

Look on the CD for more exam practice questions

❶ Examiner's tips

- You need to know about genetic diseases like cystic fibrosis and why they are passed on from generation to generation.
- You should understand why genetic modification has so much potential to treat human disease, and why there are concerns about the technique.
- You should be able to explain the potential of gene therapy in the treatment of cancer.

Can you answer these questions?

1. Why are human genetic diseases very difficult to cure?
2. Why are viruses used in gene therapy?
3. What are the risks involved in gene therapy?
4. How can gene therapy stop genetic diseases from being passed on to the next generation?

Did you know?

- Gene therapy has already been used to cure the skin cancer called malignant melanoma in two men (in 2006).

Energy flow

① Cells in close up

Have you ever wondered?

Why are plants not allowed in hospitals?

Key facts
- Animal cells contain a nucleus, cytoplasm and a cell membrane.
- Plant cells contain a nucleus, cytoplasm, and a cell membrane, as well as a vacuole, cellulose cell walls and chloroplasts.
- Chloroplasts contain the green pigment chlorophyll which is the site for **photosynthesis**.

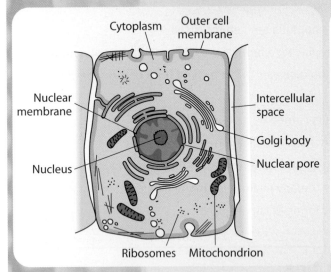

Animal cell.

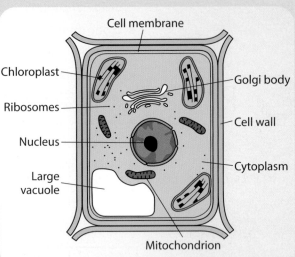

Plant cell.

- The reactants for photosynthesis are carbon dioxide (CO_2) and water (H_2O).
- The products of photosynthesis are glucose ($C_6H_{12}O_6$) and oxygen (O_2).
- The symbol equation for photosynthesis is:

$$6CO_2 + 6H_2O \rightarrow C_6H_{12}O_6 + 6O_2$$

- Photosynthesis also requires light energy and chlorophyll.

---

❶ Examiner's tips
- Ensure that you know the balanced chemical equation for photosynthesis and that the equation for respiration is the photosynthesis equation reversed.
- Plants photosynthesise when it is light but they undergo respiration at all times. Respiration takes place in the roots.
- The roots take up mineral salts by **active transport**.
- Only plants photosynthesise, animals cannot because they have no chlorophyll.
- Plants are called producers because they can produce their own food using light energy. Plants can provide more energy than animals as food sources.

Definitions

- **active transport** Movement of molecules into the cell using energy from respiration. It allows the cell to build up a high concentration of the molecules inside the cell.

- **photosynthesis** Process carried out in the green parts of plants. Carbon dioxide and water are joined to form glucose. This uses energy from sunlight.

Can you answer these questions?

1. What colour are the roots of plants? Why are they not green?
2. When does respiration occur in plants?
3. Explain why photosynthesis and respiration are reversible reactions.
4. Glucose and oxygen are produced during photosynthesis. What do these substances provide the plant with?

Look on the CD for more exam practice questions

Did you know?

- Some plants, like the Venus Fly Trap, supplement their diet by eating insects as well as photosynthesising!

② Remarkable roots

Have you ever wondered?

How can a plant make water flow upwards?

Key facts

- Photosynthesis takes place in the leaves of green plants mainly in the palisade layer.
- Not all plant cells are the same. There are specialised cells such as guard cells (these allow gases to pass into and out of the leaf) and root hair cells (for the uptake of water and minerals from the soil).

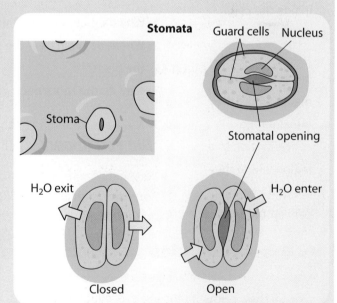

Stomata consist of two guard cells and are mainly found on the underside of the leaf.

- Minerals are absorbed through root hair cells which are elongated to give a large surface area for the uptake of water and minerals.

Water flows into the plant by **diffusion** from an area of high water concentration to an area of low water concentration. It is evaporated off the leaves, which sets up the transpiration stream and makes the water flow upwards from root to tip.

Plants take up minerals by **active transport**. This process requires energy from respiration.

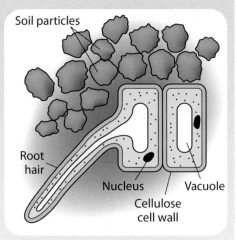

Root hair cell showing large surface area for the uptake of water and nutrients.

Definitions

- **active transport**
  Movement of molecules into the cell using energy from respiration. It allows the cell to build up a high concentration of the molecules inside the cell.

- **diffusion**
  The movement of molecules from a region where they are at a high concentration to a region where they are at a low concentration.

❶ Examiner's tips

- The minerals taken up by active transport are mainly nitrates and phosphates, these are vital to the healthy growth of the plant. Nitrates are needed for building proteins and phosphates for respiration.
- The xylem vessel carries water and minerals through the plant (this flows from root to tip).
- The phloem vessel carries glucose around the plant to where it is needed (this can flow in any direction).

Can you answer these questions?

1. Why do plants require nitrates?
2. Where do plants get the nitrates from and how are they carried through the plant?
3. Why do the roots need glucose to enable them to take up minerals?

Did you know?

- Respiration and combustion are similar reactions. Both need fuel (glucose for respiration and fossil fuels for combustion) and both need oxygen to burn the fuel to convert it into various types of energy. In both cases, carbon dioxide and water are produced.

Look on the CD for more exam practice questions

3 Controlling carbon

Have you ever wondered?

Why is there concern about **global warming**?

Key facts

- The amount of carbon dioxide in the atmosphere is crucial for keeping the temperature of the Earth stable.

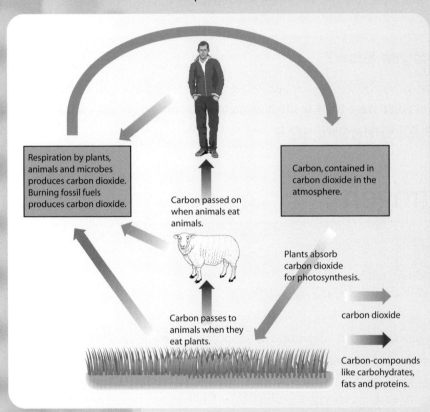

Respiration by plants, animals and microbes produces carbon dioxide. Burning fossil fuels produces carbon dioxide.

Carbon, contained in carbon dioxide in the atmosphere.

Carbon passed on when animals eat animals.

Plants absorb carbon dioxide for photosynthesis.

carbon dioxide

Carbon passes to animals when they eat plants.

Carbon-compounds like carbohydrates, fats and proteins.

The carbon cycle.

- Carbon dioxide is released by respiration, decomposition of dead organisms (plants and animals) and the burning of fossil fuels that were made millions of years ago.
- Carbon dioxide is removed from the atmosphere mainly by photosynthesis, although some dissolves into the oceans of the world as carbon dioxide is slightly soluble in water.
- Deforestation, especially in the rainforests, is reducing the number of trees and plants on Earth. This means that fewer plants are available to take in the excess carbon dioxide.
- Decomposition of plants and animals is caused by microorganisms (such as bacteria) in the soil breaking the large molecules down and releasing carbon dioxide during respiration.
- The increasing amount of carbon dioxide in the atmosphere is linked to rising global temperatures as a result of the greenhouse effect.

Definitions

- **global warming**
  The increase in the Earth's temperature that is caused by increasing amounts of greenhouse gases, such as carbon dioxide, in the atmosphere.

❶ Examiner's tips

- Fossil fuels are coal, oil and gas, which are burned to release energy.
- Electricity is *not* a clean fuel, because most electricity is produced in power plants which burn fossil fuels in order to generate electricity.
- Deforestation is being carried out in order to graze cattle, build homes or factories, and also to use the wood resources from the forests for furniture or other wood products.

Look on the CD for more exam practice questions

Can you answer these questions?

1. Why is the build up of carbon dioxide in the atmosphere thought to cause a rise in global temperatures?
2. Why are rainforests being destroyed?
3. What is the likely effect on levels of carbon dioxide in the atmosphere if rainforests continue to be destroyed?
4. What is the role of microorganisms in the soil and how do they contribute to a rise in carbon dioxide levels in the atmosphere?

Did you know?

- The carbon atoms in your body have been recycled many times. In fact, they could have been in the blue green algae which are believed to have been the first living things on Earth.

4 Natural nitrogen

Have you ever wondered?

How do fertilisers harm the environment?

Key facts

- Approximately 78% of the Earth's atmosphere is made up of nitrogen; it must be converted into **nitrates** for plants to be able to use it.
- Nitrates are found in the soil. These are used by plants and can run out.

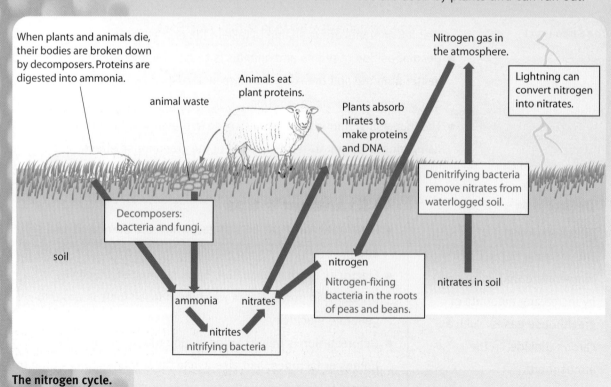

The nitrogen cycle.

- Nitrates are vital for plants because they enable them to make proteins for the growth and repair of tissue.
- Nitrogen is changed into nitrates in the soil naturally by various microorganisms.
- Decomposers break down animal waste (i.e. manure and urea) into ammonia.
- Nitrifying bacteria convert the ammonia into nitrates which plants can use.
- Some plants, such peas and beans, have nitrogen fixing bacteria on their roots. These can convert atmospheric nitrogen into nitrates for the plant to use.
- Where soil is waterlogged, denitrifying bacteria convert nitrates back into nitrogen.
- Where farmers use fields constantly, they use nitrate fertilisers to increase the quantity of nitrates in the soil which makes the plants grow quickly and healthily.
- Overuse of nitrate fertilisers can harm the environment by causing eutrophication in rivers and streams.
- Eutrophication is a build up of nitrates in rivers and streams causing excess growth of algae. This blocks out the sunlight and causes the plants under the water to die. As they decompose, oxygen is taken out of the water and, as a result, fish and insects die.

Definitions

- **nitrates**
  Chemicals used as fertilisers to make crops grow better.

❶ Examiner's tips

- Comparisons between organic farming (where no nitrate fertilisers are added but crop rotation may be used by planting peas or beans to return nitrates to the soil) and artificial farming (using nitrate fertilisers) are common areas for questions, especially the impact of each on the environment.
- The nitrogen cycle is best learnt in diagram form. Often you are asked to identify the missing bacteria or their processes.

Look on the CD for more exam practice questions

Can you answer these questions?

1. Why can nitrate fertilisers damage the environment, especially streams and rivers?
2. What can organic farmers use instead of nitrate fertilisers to put nitrates back into the soil?
3. What are two different ways in which nitrates can be converted from nitrogen in the soil?
4. What is denitrification and in what conditions does it occur?

Did you know?

- Algae growing in the wet rice fields of Asia are able to fix nitrogen directly from the air. Genetic engineers are looking for a way to move the gene for nitrogen fixing from the algae into the rice to produce rice plants that could make their own fertiliser.

⑤ Production panic

Have you ever wondered?

Why do some people put lights in greenhouses?

Key facts

- Limiting factors on plant growth are sunlight, carbon dioxide concentration, temperature and water.
- Controlling limiting factors when growing crops maximises crop yield (how much crop is produced).
- Some greenhouses are kept light for 24 hours a day so that **photosynthesis** and growth can occur continuously.
- The optimum (exactly correct) amount of water and carbon dioxide is added to maximise growth. Temperature is also kept at the optimum value.
- Artificial **fertilisers** and pesticides can increase the crop yield as less is lost due to disease or pests.
- Controlling energy loss in animals and feeding high energy food will maximise their growth.

Definitions

- **fertiliser**
  Substance added to soil that contains nutrients
- **photosynthesis**
  Process carried out in the green parts of plants. Carbon dioxide and water are joined to form glucose. This uses energy from sunlight.

Look on the CD for more exam practice questions

❶ Examiner's tips

- When looking for optimum conditions for plant growth, it is important that you can describe *why* each of these limiting factors is important. Apply each to its role in photosynthesis because this is the way in which plants release energy for growth.
- Remember that, for growth in plants, nitrates are needed to produce proteins, so your knowledge of the nitrogen cycle will also be important.
- Think of ways in which energy loss could be limited in animals. Examples are: very close living conditions, such as battery farming of chickens, to limit movement. Keeping animals in warm conditions will also limit energy loss because animals will not have to use energy to keep warm.

Can you answer these questions?

1. What are the limiting factors effecting the growth of crop plants?
2. What happens to plant growth during night time? Why would having 24-hour light improve plant growth?
3. Why are proteins important to plant growth?

Did you know?

- In some states in America 1 in 4 people is classified as obese, but millions of people in the third world are dying from starvation due to food shortages.

⑥ Population problems

Have you ever wondered?

Would it be possible to set up a **biosphere** on Mars?

Key facts

- Growing food organically could be one alternative to intensive farming.
- Organic farming methods often produce lower yield but food quality is perceived to be better and organic methods are more sustainable (we can continue to use them without depleting natural resources).
- Sustainable development means using current resources without compromising future generations.
- Alternative methods of fertilising soils such as **crop rotation** are available.
- Natural predators are an alternative to using pesticides. For example, ladybirds can be released to kill aphids on crop plants rather than killing the aphids with insecticides.
- The making of environments where plants can grow in inhospitable conditions such as deserts are being explored. Such an environment may be known as a **biosphere**.

Definitions

- **biosphere**
  A self-contained structure that holds all the plants and animals needed for a sustainable environment.
- **crop rotation**
  Changing the crop grown in fields on regular basis.

Look on the CD for more exam practice questions

❶ Examiner's tips

- When you are answering questions about intensive farming, think about both the advantages and disadvantages. Do not just use one train of thought, but apply your knowledge.
- Advantages and disadvantages of intensive farming of plant crops are:
  - fertilisers help plants grow, but there are dangers of eutrophication
  - electricity can keep plants in warm, light conditions but carbon dioxide emissions will increase
  - use of pesticides, kill off pests (weeds, insects, fungi) but effect on the food chain is unknown.
- Issues involved in intensive farming of animals are:
  - more meat produced but some people question quality (close conditions to minimise energy loss, such as fish farms and battery chicken farming, may cause disease) and animal welfare (should animals be kept in poor conditions to maximise food production?).

Can you answer these questions?

1. What is meant by the term sustainable development?
2. Describe why a consumer may prefer to buy organically grown crops in preference to intensively farmed crops.
3. Explain the advantages and disadvantages of the intensive farming of crop plants.
4. If we could make a biosphere, what may be the problems in keeping oxygen and carbon dioxide levels constant?

Interdependence

① Amazing adaptations

Have you ever wondered?

Why is there a variety of birds and not just one species?

Key facts

- Plants and animals have **adaptations** which make them more likely to be able to survive in a certain **environment**. This is linked back to Charles Darwin's theory of natural selection and the survival of the fittest.
- Those plants or animals with the best adaptations are the most likely to survive to reproduce and pass on their adaptations to their offspring.
- A predator hunts and kills another animal for food. If there are no natural predators of a species, then its numbers will grow.
- Organisms in a given environment will compete with one another for space, food, light, water and mates.
- **Interdependence** is the way in which organisms rely upon each other for food and resources. Pea and bean plants have bacteria in their roots which convert nitrogen into nitrates, and the plant provides the bacteria with nourishment in return.

Definitions

- **adaptation**
  Changing to suit the environment better.
- **environment**
  A particular set of conditions, including water, temperature, light and air.
- **interdependence**
  The mutual dependence of one organism with another.

❶ Examiner's tips

- These questions appear easy to answer but you must answer them fully. Many marks are lost by incomplete answers.
- For adaptations questions, ensure you relate the structure to its nature and its function. Polar bears have small ears, so have a small surface area which reduces heat loss. All of these points are needed for a mark.
- Predator/prey graphs often appear. Remember that the predators are always fewer than the prey. Remember also that the predator numbers will mirror the prey numbers but with a slight delay.

Can you answer these questions?

1. How is the snow leopard adapted to its environment?
2. How is an angel fish adapted to living in the ocean? (Include gills, scales, shape, as well as the stripes on the body.)
3. For what does a rabbit compete with other rabbits in the environment?
4. Why do plants produce beautifully coloured flowers? What are they competing for?

Look on the CD for more exam practice questions

Did you know?

- Dandelion plants actually release toxins into the environment to inhibit the growth of other plants in the area. This reduces competition.

2 Extreme environments

Have you ever wondered?

Can organisms live in an oxygen free environment?

Key facts

- Many animals and plants are specially adapted for the environment in which they live, such as deserts, Antarctica and deep sea hydrothermal vents.
- All organisms need certain things to survive. These are: a source of energy, water, the correct temperature, and (for *almost* all), oxygen.
- Organisms found in hydrothermal vents live off the minerals which are given off from black smokers (underwater vents in the Earth's crust). These organisms are the first we are aware of that do not rely on sunlight as their ultimate energy source.
- Desert environments lead to organisms being adapted to retain water, for example, the camel and the cactus. The cactus does not have leaves but spines which reduce the water loss from the plant. They also have an extensive root system to enable them to reach deep underground for water.
- **Extreme environments**, such as Antarctica, can have temperatures down to −70 °C. Penguins have adapted to this environment by having a thick layer of fat insulation and an extra layer of downy feathers to enable them to withstand the harsh environment.
- By studying fossil evidence and the adaptations of the animals and plants in these harsh environments, we get a clearer idea of the way in which evolution occurs.

Definitions

- **extreme environment**
  Conditions that are far outside the boundaries in which humans can live comfortably.

❶ Examiner's tips

- When reading questions about extreme environments, note the information you are given. You are not expected to know what every environment is like, but you should be able to draw conclusions based on the information you are given.
- Think about why certain adaptations may be useful and in what type of environment.
- Hydrothermal vents are a very popular question area because there are so many unusual organisms that examiners can compose questions about.

Look on the CD for more exam practice questions

Can you answer these questions?

1. The vent crab is a good swimmer, has infrared vision (to see in the dark), has a good sense of smell and can adapt to very low and very high temperatures. How do these adaptations suit it to life in deep ocean hydrothermal vents?

2. Give two examples of extreme environments and how organisms are adapted to living there.

Did you know?

- Penguins waddle because they cannot bend their knees.

③ Challenging competition

Have you ever wondered?

If animals fight over mating partners, what do plants fight over?

Key facts

- Animals and plants compete for resources (food for animals, light for plants), space and mates.
- Intraspecific competition is between members of the same species.
- Interspecific competition is between members of different species.
- Humans generally win in interspecific competition with other species, usually as a result of technology, but this can have devastating effects on the **biodiversity** of an area.
- Human demand for resources and space from the environment has led to air and water pollution. This has further reduced plant and animal populations.
- Air pollution is caused by soot and other chemicals, such as carbon dioxide and sulphur dioxide, as a result of burning fossil fuels.
- Water pollution is caused as a result of sewage, and nitrate and phosphate build up in rivers and streams.
- As a result of air pollution there have been rises in the dark peppered moth population and reductions in the light peppered moth population because the dark type is more camouflaged in the dark, polluted environment of cities.
- As a result of water pollution, acid rain has affected organisms in lakes, which changes the biodiversity of the environment.

Definitions

● biodiversity
A measure of the variety of species of plants and animals.

Look on the CD for more exam practice questions

❶ Examiner's tips

- When describing human influence on the environment, ensure your facts do not get mixed up. Damage to the ozone layer is *not* the same as global warming.
- Acid rain is a result of sulphur dioxide and nitrogen oxides dissolving in rain water.
- Try to relate your answers not simply to the effect of pollution on humans, but also on the environment itself. Always avoid statements such as 'It harms the environment.'

Can you answer these questions?

1. What may be the effects of more harmful ultraviolet radiation getting through to the Earth's surface?
2. What may be a result of the build up of nitrates and phosphates in rivers and streams? (See p. 27.)
3. Why is the dark coloured peppered moth more adapted to city living than the light coloured peppered moth?

Did you know?

- The ozone layer is a layer surrounding the Earth which acts to prevent harmful ultraviolet rays reaching to the Earth's surface. Ozone is O_3, this is oxygen bonded in groups of three. The ozone layer is depleted by harmful chemicals such as CFCs (chlorofluorocarbons) formerly released from some packaging, aerosols and refrigerators.

④ Plastic pollutants

Have you ever wondered?

Why is it important to recycle materials?

Key facts

- Plastics now make up about 7% of our household waste, that is, nearly 3 million tons per year.
- Many plastics are made from the raw material crude oil, which is also used to produce fossil fuels such as petrol, diesel and kerosene.
- Most plastics do not break down in the environment (they are non-biodegradable). Therefore they take up a large proportion of space in landfill sites.
- Plastic waste should not be incinerated (burnt) as it releases toxic gases into the environment.
- More research is going into making biodegradable plastics or plastics which are recyclable.

- The **recycling** of glass uses more than 50% less energy than producing new glass.
- The recycling of steel uses 75% less energy than producing new steel. There is also a major reduction in the amount of carbon dioxide produced.

Definitions

- **recycling**
  Reusing materials instead of additional original resources.

Look on the CD for more exam practice questions

❶ Examiner's tips

- Most questions will be based around the advantages of recycling or reasons why we should recycle more. Do not fall into the trap of giving a vague answer, i.e. is saves money or produces less pollution. Be specific about why plastics are a particular problem. Biodegradable is a key word for you to use.

Can you answer these questions?

1. Britain is one of the worst countries in Europe for recycling. Why do you think fewer people recycle in Britain than in other European countries?
2. Give three reasons why plastics should be used less for packaging until it can be made to be recyclable.
3. When many products decay in landfill sites they give off carbon dioxide and methane. Why is this another reason to recycle rather than use landfill?

Did you know?

- The mass of carbon dioxide in the atmosphere is currently increasing across the world by about 6100 million tonnes per year.

⑤ Deciphering data

Have you ever wondered?

How fast are humans destroying the environment?

❶ Examiner's tips

- It is vitally important that you are able to decipher data on the environment effectively.
- Pie charts give values of data, sometimes as a percentage. The largest piece of the pie is the biggest source.
- Bar charts are simple to read. The largest bars have the biggest effects. Line graphs often show several pieces of data at once. Make sure you read off the correct axis. Time scale in years is almost always plotted along the *x*-axis (horizontal).

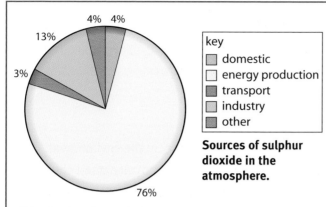

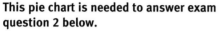

Sources of sulphur dioxide in the atmosphere.

This pie chart is needed to answer exam question 2 below.

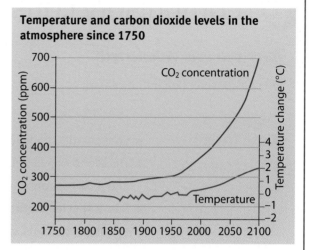

- A very popular set of questions are based around temperature and carbon dioxide level graphs. Be careful that you read off the correct scale because there are two *y*-axis (vertical axis) scales. The temperature usually runs up one side and the carbon dioxide levels on the other. Time in years again is along the *x*-axis.
- Be careful with questions which ask you to make assumptions based on limited data.

Worked example

Use the graph above entitled 'Temperature and carbon dioxide levels in the atmosphere since 1750'.

1. How does this graph show a correlation between carbon dioxide levels and increase in global temperature? (2 Marks)

   The patterns of both show a positive correlation in line with one another.

   As carbon dioxide levels rise, so do global temperatures. (1 mark)

   This graph is over too long a period of time to show this.

   It does show increasing carbon dioxide levels in recent time but more information about the past 100 years is necessary to answer this question. (1 mark)

2. Does the graph show a rise in global temperature levels? If so, can this all be attributed to the rise in carbon dioxide levels in the atmosphere? (2 Marks)

   The rise is slight, however the predicted rise is much greater. (1 Mark)

   More information is needed regarding the rise in temperature.

   Although a correlation appears to exist, further evidence would be needed to make a categorical statement. (1 Mark)

Look on the CD for more exam practice questions

Can you answer these questions?

1. What are the carbon dioxide levels in the year 1950?
2. Using the pie chart above, what is the largest source of sulphur dioxide in the atmosphere? What environmental problem does it cause?
3. What is the predicted temperature change by the year 2100, based on the graph?
4. How does the graph show that global temperature is related to the carbon dioxide levels in the atmosphere?

Compulsory conservation

Have you ever wondered?

Why all conservation initiatives are not equally successful?

Key facts

- Conservation is developed to maintain biodiversity in the environment.
- The World Conservation Union monitors populations of all natural species and it has produced a red list of endangered species.
- Some species on the endangered list have been successfully reintroduced to natural habitats and have bred in the wild.
- Coppicing is a technique where trees like hazel and willow are cut near the base of their trunks, this encourages new branches to grow very quickly.
- Reforestation is the replanting of trees on areas where there used to be large forests. This increases the habitat for plants and animals, stabilises the soil and increases air quality.
- Replacement planting is where a plant or shrub is removed and replaced by a plant of the same species nearby. This encourages the biodiversity of the area to continue.

Definitions

- **recycling**
  Reusing materials instead of additional original resources.

Look on the CD for more exam practice questions

❶ Examiner's tips

- Biodiversity does not only mean the animals in a given habitat but also the plants.
- Remember, biodiversity is not the numbers of animals or plants but the number of different species of plants or animals.
- Methods of conservation are designed to combat changes that humans have made to their environment. Natural changes are known as succession. Conservation techniques sometimes stop these natural changes from happening to preserve the current environment.

Can you answer these questions?

1. Why is it important to retain the biodiversity in the environment?
2. Name three conservation techniques designed to maintain biodiversity.
3. What is the difference between succession and conservation?
4. What is the function of The World Conservation Union? What does it seek to promote?

Did you know?

- Two out of every five species on the planet that have been assessed by scientists are facing extinction.

Synthesis

1 Cracking and reforming

Have you ever wondered?

How are plastics made from oil?

Key facts

- Most plastics are made from oil.
- Oil was formed millions of years ago from dead sea creatures.
- Once the oil has been extracted from the Earth or sea, the first stage in refining it is fractional distillation.
- It can be changed further by **cracking** and reforming.
- The simplest group of organic compounds is the **alkanes**.
- Cracking breaks down bigger hydrocarbon molecules into smaller, more useful molecules. One of the most useful is ethene, which is one of the **alkenes**.
- Alkene molecules have at least one double bond between two carbon atoms. Alkane molecules have only single bonds.

Definitions

- **alkane**
  A hydrocarbon in which all the bonds between the carbon atoms are single bonds.
- **alkene**
  A hydrocarbon in which two or more carbon atoms are joined by double bonds.
- **cracking** A type of chemical reaction in which large alkane molecules are decomposed to form smaller alkanes and alkenes.

❶ Examiner's tips

- You can work out the formulae for members of the alkane and alkene families if you know the general formulae. These are:
  alkanes C_nH_{2n+2} alkenes C_nH_{2n} where n is the number of atoms of carbon in the molecule.

Can you answer these questions?

1. Why does crude oil have to be fractionally distilled, rather than undergo simple distillation?
2. If cracking breaks down big molecules, suggest what reforming might do.
3. Explain the difference between alkanes and alkenes.
4. Here are the molecular formulae for the first three members of the alkane series: CH_4, C_2H_6, C_3H_8. What is the molecular formula for the next member of the series?
5. Draw the structural formula of the first member of the alkene series. It has 2 carbon atoms.

Look on the CD for more exam practice questions

Did you know?

- Crude oil is difficult to ignite.
- Crude oil contains hundreds of different chemical substances.
- Bromine water can be used to distinguish between alkanes and alkenes.

② Saturated and unsaturated

Have you ever wondered?

How do we make enough petrol for all the cars in the world given that the fractional distillation of crude oil produces only a small amount of petrol?

Key facts

- The formula for ethene is C_2H_4.
- Each molecule of ethene contains one double bond between the two carbon atoms. This is what gives it its chemically reactivity.
- Ethene is an example of an unsaturated hydrocarbon.
- Ethanol can be made by reacting ethene with steam.
- Small alkene molecules, such as ethene, can be made to join together in long chains to form much bigger molecules.

$$
\begin{array}{ccccccc}
H & H & & H & H & & H & H \\
| & | & & | & | & & | & | \\
C & = & C & \quad C & = & C & \quad C & = & C & \longrightarrow \\
| & | & & | & | & & | & | \\
H & H & & H & H & & H & H
\end{array}
$$

- These very large molecules are called **polymers**.
- The polymer made by joining many ethene molecules is called poly(ethene), (or more commonly just polythene). Poly(ethene) is a saturated hydrocarbon, because it contains no double bonds, only single bonds.
- The small alkene molecules are sometimes called **monomers**.
- Polymers can be made of several thousand atoms.

Definitions

- **monomer** A small molecule, that can be joined to many other small molecules to form a much larger molecule.
- **polymer** Large molecule made by linking together many small molecules (monomers).

❶ Examiner's tips

- Make sure that you know the difference between an alkane and an alkene.
- Starting from three molecules of ethene, you should be able to show how they can join together to make part of the polymer poly(ethene).
- You should be able to name other monomers apart from ethene.

Look on the CD for more exam practice questions

Can you answer these questions?

1. Why do you think a molecule of ethene may be termed a monomer?
2. Can a molecule of ethane (C_2H_6) be termed a monomer? Explain your answer.
3. Styrene is the old name for phenylethene. What is (a) the old name for the polymer formed from styrene (b) the new name for this polymer?

Did you know?

- Shopping bags are normally made of poly(ethene).

③ Types of polymers

Have you ever wondered?

How do you make slime balls?

Key facts

- There are two main types of polymer:
  - **thermoplastic**, which softens on heating, and
  - **thermosetting**, which sets hard on manufacture, and cannot be melted again.
- Polymers may be **addition** polymers (which are formed when simple molecules add together to form a long chain), or condensation polymers (which are formed when monomer molecules link together, with the elimination of small molecules such as water or hydrogen chloride).
- Thermosetting plastics have crosslinks between the polymer chains. This is what makes them rigid. An example is the material used for electrical plug casings and sockets.
- Milk crates are made from high density poly(ethene) (which has few branches in its chains), a plastic ruler may be made from low density poly(ethene) (which has many branches in its chains).

Definitions

- **addition** In polymer chemistry, a large molecule formed from alkene molecules added together to form chains.
- **thermoplastic** A polymer that softens or melts when heated and becomes hard again when cooled.
- **thermosetting** A polymer that cannot be melted or remoulded again once formed.

❶ Examiner's tips

- Chemists can change the properties of polymers, for example, by crosslinking the molecules, adding preservatives and adding plasticisers.

Look on the CD for more exam practice questions

Can you answer these questions?

1. Why do you think it is easier to recycle thermoplastics than thermosetting plastics?
2. Plastic window frames may be made of uPVC. What does the 'u' stand for and what is the chemical name for PVC ?
3. Can you find the name of a common condensation polymer used to make clothing?

Did you know?

- Slime balls may be made from the reaction between PVA glue (polyvinyl alcohol) and borax.
- Some plastics are now 'biodegradeable'.

④ It's all fat, but does it make you fat?

Have you ever wondered?

What is the difference between 'total fat' and 'saturated fat' on food labels?

Key facts

- There is little difference between a fat and an oil. Oils are normally liquid at room temperatures, whereas fats are usually solids.
- Vegetable oils, such as rapeseed, sunflower and olive oil, are used for cooking and to make margarine.
- Margarine is made by reacting vegetable oils with hydrogen, which reacts with the double bonds in molecules of the oils. Complete **hydrogenation** results in saturated molecules only, but margarines can be made by partial hydrogenation, which results in a mixture of saturated and unsaturated molecules.
- Margarine has low levels of saturated fats and contains no cholesterol.

Definitions

- **hydrogenate** To add hydrogen to a molecule by a chemical reaction.
- **monounsaturated** A substance (usually a fat) that only has one double bond.
- **polyunsaturated** A substance (usually a fat) that has more than one double bond.

❶ Examiner's tips

- Find out about triesters of propan-1,2,3 triol and their importance in margarine manufacture.
- Find out about cholesterol and the importance of maintaining a low level of it in the bloodstream to reduce the risk of a heart attack.

Look on the CD for more exam practice questions

Can you answer these questions?

1. What is the difference between a margarine which is rich in **polyunsaturates** and one which contains mainly **monounsaturates**?
2. If you are trying to reduce your blood cholesterol levels, should you use butter or margarine in your sandwiches and on your toast?
3. Why are polyunsaturated oils thinner than saturated ones?

Did you know?

- Butter contains about 85% butterfats and 15% water.
- Butter contains high levels of saturated fats and cholesterol.
- Margarine was named after the Greek word for pearl, *margaron*.
- The first margarine was made in Europe in 1878.

5 Making new chemicals

Have you ever wondered?

How do chemists discover new drugs?

Key facts

- Bottles containing toxic substances should be labelled with the appropriate hazard symbol.
- Newly-discovered substances are tested for **toxicity** before they are released to the public.
- Synthesis is the name given to the manufacture of a substance from its starting materials.
- Computer modelling and tests on cells grown in the laboratory are common ways of testing new chemical substances.
- Chemists use their existing knowledge of substances to predict properties of new substances.
- The synthesis of a drug can involve several stages from the starting materials to the final product. The nature of the reactions in these stages is a major factor in the cost of production.
- At each stage in the production of a new drug, new products are made and these all need to be tested. Such a synthesis is called staged synthesis.
- Processes which have a high atom economy are more efficient than those with low atom economy.

Definitions

- **toxicity** How toxic or poisonous a substance is. Very toxic substances have a high toxicity.

❶ Examiner's tips

- The formula:

$$\frac{\text{mass of useful product}}{\text{total mass of reactants}} \times 100\%$$

can be used to calculate the atom economy of a reaction.

Look on
the CD
for more
exam
practice
questions

Can you answer these questions?

1. In a certain synthesis reaction there are three stages. In stage 1 there are three products. Each product from stage 1 can form two products in stage 2. Each product from stage 2 can form three products in stage 3.

   (a) How many products are made in stage 3?

   (b) How many products are made in total in all three stages – assuming that every product is different?

⑥ Using chemical reactions

Have you ever wondered?

How do chemists know how much starting material to use to produce the required amount of product ?

Key facts

- Elements have different relative atomic masses. For example, H = 1, O = 16, C = 12, etc. This is because atoms of each element contain different numbers of particles.
- One molecule of carbon dioxide has the formula CO_2. This means that one molecule contains one carbon atom and two oxygen atoms combined together.
- The **relative formula** (or molecular) **mass** of carbon dioxide is therefore 12 + $(16 \times 2) = 44$.
- The chemical equation Fe + S → FeS enables us to calculate that 56 g of iron will react with 32 g of sulphur to make 88 g of iron II sulphide. Check the atomic masses.
- Suppose we had 5.6 g of iron. It would react with 3.2 g sulphur to form 8.8 g of iron II sulphide.
- We can use **relative atomic masses** to work out formulae. If we know what mass of each substance combines to make a compound, we can work out the formula of that compound.
- Although we can work out in this way how much of a product should be formed, experimentally less product is formed. The actual yield is less than the **theoretical yield**.

Definitions

- **relative atomic mass** The mass of an atom compared to one twelfth of the mass of a carbon atom, which has a relative atomic mass of 12. Abbreviated to A_r.
- **relative formula mass** The mass of a molecule relative to one twelfth of the mass of a carbon atom. Abbreviated to M_r.
- **theoretical yield** The maximum calculated amount of product that can be obtained from a particular quantity of reactants. Also called expected yield.

Look on the CD for more exam practice questions

❶ Examiner's tips

- Make sure you know the difference between relative atomic and formula or molecular mass. (In general atomic masses refer to elements and formula (and molecular) mass refer to compounds.)

Can you answer these questions?

1. What are the relative atomic masses for sodium, chlorine, calcium, potassium and bromine ?
2. Work out the relative formula masses for these compounds: NaCl, KCl, $CaBr_2$, NaBr, KBr.
3. Using this equation $H_2 + Cl_2 \rightarrow 2HCl$, what is the maximum mass of hydrogen chloride than can be formed when an excess of hydrogen reacts with 7.1. g of chlorine?
4. What is the minimum mass of calcium carbonate required to make 112 tonnes of calcium oxide? $CaCo_3 \rightarrow CaO + CO_2$ (Relative atomic masses Ca = 40, C = 12, O = 16).

Did you know?

- In 12g of carbon powder there are more than 6×10^{23} or 600 000 000 000 000 000 000 000 atoms.

In your element

1 The properties of metals

Have you ever wondered?

What is the difference between 9 and 18 carat gold?

Key facts

- Most metals are shiny, **malleable**, ductile and they are all good conductors of electricity. They have many uses.
- The properties of metals can be explained by understanding how their atoms are bonded together.
- Metals conduct electricity because the outer electrons of their atoms are not strongly held in position. These electrons can move and carry the electric current.
- Alloys are mixtures of metals. Alloying changes the properties of the individual metals. Shape memory alloys are used for modern spectacle frames, which can be bent into different shapes but always return to the original shape when the force is no longer applied.
- Alloying mixes atoms of other elements into the structure of the original metal to make it stronger, harder or more resistant to corrosion. For example, a few copper or manganese atoms alloyed with aluminium makes aluminium much stronger (though it still has a low density) and so the alloy can be used for aircraft bodies.

Definitions

- **malleable** Can be bent or hammered into shape without breaking.

Look on the CD for more exam practice questions

❶ Examiner's tips

- You should be aware that there are many different metal alloys in use today.

Can you answer these questions?

1. What are the natural patterns you can sometimes see on metal lamp-posts?
2. Magnets can be made of the alloy alnico. What three elements do you think an alnico magnet contains?
3. Find out what metals are present in the alloy duralumin.

Did you know?

- Brass and bronze are two alloys that have been known since ancient times.

② Atoms of elements

Have you ever wondered?

Should we think of an atom as a solid sphere?

Key facts

- Until the early part of the last century people thought atoms were single particles which could not be split up.
- Now it is known that atoms are mostly empty space and most atoms contain three basic particles: protons, neutrons and electrons.
- Different atoms contain different numbers of these three subatomic particles.
- Each atom has a nucleus. This is at the centre of the atom and contains all the protons and neutrons present in the atom.
- The electrons surround the nucleus and, at normal temperatures, are continually moving.
- Protons are positively charged, electrons are negatively charged and neutrons have no charge.
- To make things simple, we say the proton has a charge of +1 and the electron has a charge of −1.
- The subatomic particles have masses, but as their masses are very small, we refer to their relative masses rather than their actual masses.
- The relative masses used are proton = 1, neutron = 1, electron = $\frac{1}{1837}$ (negligible).

Definitions

- **atomic number**
  The number of protons (positively charged particles) in the nucleus of an atom.
- **mass number**
  The total number of protons and neutrons in the nucleus of an atom. Also called nucleon number.

Look on the CD for more exam practice questions

❶ Examiner's tips

- Remember that the relative charges and relative masses given above have no units.
- We can use the atomic symbol with **mass number** and **atomic number** to state the number of subatomic particles in the atom. For example, the symbol $^{7}_{3}$Li tells us that a lithium atom has 3 protons, 3 electrons and 4 neutrons.

Can you answer these questions?

1. Where in the atom is almost all of the mass to be found?
2. How is the atom of oxygen different from the atom of nitrogen?
3. How many protons, neutrons and electrons are in $^{23}_{11}$Na ?

Did you know?

- The history of our knowledge of the structure of the atom is fascinating. Look up what these scientists contributed to our knowledge of atomic structure: Dalton, Thomson, Rutherford, Bohr, Newlands.

3 Electron arrangements

Have you ever wondered?

What makes, for example, platinum, diamond and zirconium look so different, when they're all made from protons, neutrons and electrons?

Key facts

- All the atoms of any particular element have the same number of protons in their atoms and this is different from the number of protons in the atoms of any other element.
- The electrons surround the nucleus and are arranged in orbits (or shells).
- The first orbit closest to the nucleus is smallest, and can contain a maximum of two electrons. The next orbit contains a maximum of eight electrons.
- The alkali metals (lithium, sodium, potassium, rubidium, and caesium) are so reactive because they only have one electron in their outer orbit (shell).
- Diagrams such as the one above, show the arrangement of the electrons in an atom. The potassium atom has the electronic configuration 2, 8, 8, 1.
- When similar diagrams are drawn for the elements in the periodic table, some interesting patterns emerge.

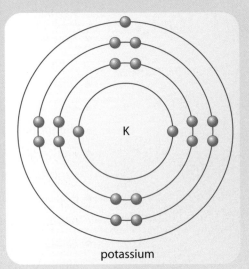

potassium

The electrons in a potassium atom.

Definitions

- **electronic configuration**
  The arrangement of electrons in shells around the nucleus.

❶ Examiner's tips

- Remember that the number of electrons in any atom must always equal the number of protons in the nucleus and therefore is the same as the atomic number of the element.

Can you answer these questions?

1. How many electrons are there in an atom of potassium?
2. What is the connection between the electronic arrangement in an atom of an element and the element's group number in the periodic table?
3. What are the electronic arrangements in these atoms: sodium, magnesium, carbon, and argon?

Look on the CD for more exam practice questions

Did you know?

● The elements fluorine and neon have very different properties but, in terms of their atomic structure, the only differences between their commonest atoms are 1 proton and 1 electron!

④ Ions and ionic bonding

Have you ever wondered?

What is an ion?

Key facts

● Sometimes atoms of different elements combine by losing or gaining electrons. They do this in order to completely remove, or fill up, their partially full outer electron orbits.

● The particles formed usually have eight electrons in their outer shells (only two if it is the first shell).

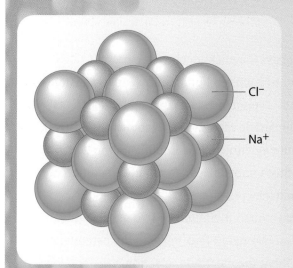

The ionic structure of sodium chloride.

● When electrons are lost or gained, the particles produced have a positive or negative charge, and are called **ions**.

● Metals (and hydrogen) form positively-charged ions, non-metals form negatively-charged ions.

● It is mainly elements from groups 1, 2, 3, 6, and 7 that form ions.

● When oppositely charged ions attract each other, giant ionic lattices are formed. The resulting crystals have flat faces and sharp edges.

● Substances which have **ionic bonds** do not conduct electricity when they are solid, but they do when dissolved in water or when molten.

Definitions

● **ion** An atom or group of atoms with an electrical charge.

● **ionic bonds** Force between oppositely charged ions.

❶ Examiner's tips

● Sodium chloride does not exist as a simple molecule of NaCl. A sodium chloride crystal is a giant ionic lattice made of many Na^+ ions and Cl^- ions. If you look through a hand lens, you can clearly see the flat faces and sharp edges of each individual crystal.

Look on the CD for more exam practice questions

Can you answer these questions?

1. What are the formulae of the ions of these elements: potassium, bromine, oxygen, sulphur, lithium, iodine, and magnesium?
2. Why does an ionic solid not conduct electricity?
3. Complete these ionic half equations:

   (a) $Ca \rightarrow ... + 2e^-$ (b) $Rb \rightarrow ... + e^-$

   (c) $I + ... \rightarrow I^-$ (d) $H \rightarrow H^+ + ...$

Did you know?

- The reason that ionic compounds conduct electricity when dissolved in water (or when molten) is that the ionic structure breaks down and the ions become free to move and carry the current.

⑤ Electrolysis

Have you ever wondered?

How does hair removal by electrolysis work?

Key facts

- Electrolysis is a chemical process in which an electric current is used to decompose either a solution, or a molten liquid, into simpler substances.
- Direct (not alternating) electric current must be used.
- The two **electrodes**, called the anode (positive) and cathode (negative), pass the electricity through the electrolyte (the liquid).
- Electrolytes must be one of these substances: an aqueous solution of an acid, alkali or salt or molten alkalis or salts.
- The electric current is carried through the liquid by free moving ions.
- During electrolysis, metal (and hydrogen) ions move to the cathode, non-metal ions move to the anode. At the electrode, electron transfer takes place to form the product.
- Half equations are used to show the reactions at the two electrodes.
- The products of electrolysis are usually gases, or metals (which are deposited on the cathode).
- There are many applications of electrolysis, from its use in hairdressing salons, to important industrial processes such as the electrolysis of sodium hydroxide solution (which produces hydrogen, chlorine and sodium hydroxide) and in the coating of dull metals with bright shiny chromium.

Definitions

- **electrode** A rod of conductive material used in electrolysis.

❶ Examiner's tips

- The electrolysis of a binary salt is commonly used to test understanding in exam questions.
- Common binary salts are lead bromide and copper chloride.

Look on the CD for more exam practice questions

Can you answer these questions?

1. Why must the salt lead bromide be molten in order to undergo electrolysis?
2. When copper chloride is electrolysed, what will be the product at (a) the anode (b) the cathode?
3. (a) Complete this half equation: $Pb^{2+} + \ldots \rightarrow Pb$
   (b) At which electrode would this reaction take place?

Did you know?

- During hair removal by electrolysis, a hair-thin metal probe is slid into a hair follicle. Electricity is delivered to the follicle through the probe, which causes localised damage to the areas that generate hairs.

6 Isotopes and relative atomic mass

Have you ever wondered?

How do scientists detect new elements (such as the element with atomic number 115) if they only last milliseconds before disintegrating?

Key facts

- Although all of the atoms of a given element must have the same number of protons (and electrons), different atoms of the same element can have different numbers of neutrons in their nuclei. Such atoms are called **isotopes**.
- Isotopes of the same element must have the same atomic number but because they have different numbers of neutrons, they have different **mass numbers**.
- Isotopes are named after their mass number. For example, hydrogen-1, (normal hydrogen, protium) hydrogen-2 (deuterium), and hydrogen-3 (tritium).
- On some copies of the periodic table, the relative atomic masses of elements are given to several places of decimals. This is mainly because the relative atomic mass of an element is an average of the relative masses of all of the isotopes of that element present in a normal sample.
- For example there are two isotopes of chlorine – chlorine 35, and chlorine 37. It just so happens that 75% of all of the atoms of chlorine are chlorine 35, and 25% are chlorine 37. So the average relative atomic mass is
$$\frac{3 \times 35}{4} + \frac{1 \times 37}{4} = 35.5$$

Definitions

- **isotopes** Atoms of an element with the same number of protons and electrons but different numbers of neutrons.
- **mass number** The total number of protons and neutrons in the nucleus of an atom. Also called nucleon number.

Look on the CD for more exam practice questions

❶ Examiner's tips

- Calculations on the isotopes of chlorine are frequently set as an exam question to test your understanding of isotopes.

Can you answer these questions?

1. How many protons, neutrons and electrons are there in each of the three isotopes of hydrogen?
2. Describe the structure of the two atoms: $^{12}_{6}C$ $^{14}_{6}C$
3. If 60% of the atoms of an element have mass number 42 and the rest have a mass number of 48, calculate the average relative atomic mass of that element to one decimal place.

Did you know?

- Hydrogen has 7 isotopes. Two of these are stable and 5 are unstable.

Chemical structures

1 Covalent bonding

Key facts

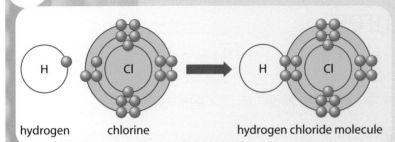

hydrogen   chlorine   hydrogen chloride molecule

Covalent bonds shown by electron shells.

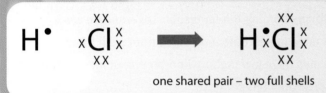

one shared pair – two full shells

Covalent bonds shown by dot and cross diagrams.

- Non-metals form covalent bonds by sharing electrons.
- When forming covalent bonds, atoms usually obtain eight electrons in their outer shells to have an electronic configuration like noble gases.
- The outer electron shell for hydrogen can hold just two electrons.
- The outer electron shell for other non-metals can hold eight electrons.
- Covalent molecules are formed when two or more atoms share electrons.
- Metals and noble gases usually do not form covalent bonds.
- We can show covalent bonds with dot and cross diagrams or by drawing electron shells.

Definitions

- **covalent bond**
  A chemical bond that forms when two atoms share a pair of electrons.

❗ Examiner's tips

- A hydrogen atom can only share one electron and form one covalent bond.
- All gases except noble gases have covalent molecules.

Group	Number of outer electrons	Number of shared electrons	Number of bonds formed
4	4	4	4
5	5	3	3
6	6	2	2
7	7	1	1

Can you answer these questions?

1. What happens to the electrons in a covalent bond?
2. Name three covalent gases.
3. Oxygen is a group 6 element.
   (a) How many electrons are in its outer shell?
   (b) How many covalent bonds can it form?
4. Which of these is not a covalent compound?
   H_2O, CO_2, HCl, NaCl

Look on the CD for more exam practice questions

Did you know?

- An American scientist, Gilbert Newton Lewis, first suggested the electron dot diagrams for covalent bonding in 1916.

② Simple structures

Have you ever wondered?

Do the essential oils that supermarkets spray into the air put you in a positive mood?

Key facts

- Small covalent molecules are simple molecular structures.
- The covalent bonds between atoms are very strong.
- The **inter-molecular forces** holding the molecules together are weak.
- It takes only a little energy to separate molecules from each other.
- Small covalent molecules have low melting and boiling points. They are often gases or liquids at room temperature.
- Solid, small covalent molecules like iodine are soft and do not conduct electricity.

Definitions

- **halogen** An family of reactive non-metals found in Group 7 of the periodic table.
- **inter-molecular force** The force of attraction between molecules.

❶ Examiner's tips

- Molecules have no overall charge.
- The smaller the molecule, the lower the melting and boiling points.
- Small covalent compounds like perfume evaporate easily.
- **Halogens** form small covalent molecules.
- Simple covalent molecules usually dissolve in organic solvents not water.

Can you answer these questions?

1. Which of these is stronger?
   (a) an inter-molecular force or (b) a covalent bond
2. What is the charge on an ammonia molecule?
3. When ice melts, what happens to
   (a) the atoms   (b) the molecules?
4. Why is it important that perfume is made of small covalent compounds?

Look on the CD for more exam practice questions

Did you know?

- Sulphur forms a molecule with a zigzag ring of eight atoms.

③ Giant molecular structures

Have you ever wondered?

Why are diamonds so expensive when scientists can create them in a few hours?

Key facts

- Some covalent molecules form **giant covalent structures** of millions of atoms called macromolecules.
- Each carbon atom in **diamond** forms four covalent bonds with other carbon atoms in a 3-D pattern.
- Germanium and silicon have the same structure as diamond.
- Covalent bonds are strong, so a lot of energy (a high temperature) is needed to melt giant molecular structures.
- Giant molecular structures are hard solids that do not conduct electricity (except for graphite).

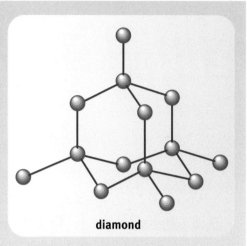

diamond

Definitions

- **diamond** A very hard, natural form of carbon which has a 3-D giant covalent structure in which every atom is joined to four neighbours.
- **giant covalent structure** A structure built from billions of atoms in which every atom is joined to its neighbours by strong covalent bonds.

❶ Examiner's tips

- Giant molecular structures do not dissolve in water or organic solvents.
- You should be able to draw the diamond structure.
- Ice and silicon dioxide can form similar structures to diamond.

Can you answer these questions?

1. What is the type of bonding in silicon dioxide?
2. Why is the melting point of silicon dioxide so high (about 1700 °C)?
3. Explain why diamond is hard.
4. Why are giant molecular structures difficult to cut?

Look on the CD for more exam practice questions

Did you know?

- Ice can have eight other giant molecular structures which will sink, not float in water.

4 Giant metallic structures

Key facts

- Metals form giant structures of many millions of atoms.
- The nuclei and inner electrons form a close packed lattice of positive ions.
- The outermost electrons form a negative 'cloud' throughout the lattice which gives it its **conductivity**.
- These electrons can move and conduct electricity and heat.
- The force of attraction between the positive ions and the negative electrons holds the solid together.
- This metallic bond is strong so metals have high melting and boiling points.
- Metals are malleable and ductile.
- When metals are hot, the ions vibrate, making it harder for the electrons to move.

Definitions

- **conductivity**
  A property of a substance that describes its ability to allow energy (electricity or heat) to pass through it.

Look on the CD for more exam practice questions

❶ Examiner's tips

- Very cold metals can form superconductors.
- Adding a small amount of another metal as an impurity makes a metal stronger, but not as good a conductor.
- An alloy is a mixture of two or more metals.

Can you answer these questions?

1. How do metals conduct?
2. What do these terms mean
   (a) malleable   (b) ductile   (c) thermal conductor?
3. Which are the best conditions for good electrical conduction?
   (a) cold with impurities in the metal
   (b) cold without impurities in the metal
   (c) hot with impurities in the metal
   (d) hot without impurities in the metal.
4. Why do we add silver and copper to gold used for jewellery?

Did you know?

- The ancient Romans and Greeks only knew of seven metals; today we know over 80.

5 Carbon structures

Have you ever wondered?

Why is life on Earth based on the carbon atom?

Key facts

- Carbon forms four covalent bonds.
- Carbon can form different structures. For example, diamond, graphite, carbon nanotubes.
- Diamond has a very strong 3-D lattice structure with each atom bonding to four others.
- Graphite has layers of hexagons where each atom bonds to three others.
- The 'unused' electrons in graphite form an electron cloud between the layers so graphite can conduct.
- Buckminster fullerene has 60 atoms arranged in pentagons and hexagons just like a football.
- Nanotubes are incredibly tiny layers of graphite rolled into tubes.

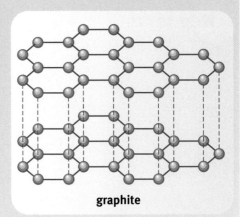

graphite

Definitions

- **buckminster fullerene** A form of carbon in which graphite-like sheets of carbon atoms form balls or tubes.
- **carbon nanotube** A type of Buckminster fullerene in which the sheet structures of carbon atoms are rolled into very thin tubes. Also called buckytubes.
- **graphite** A very soft, natural form of carbon which has a sheet-like giant covalent structure in which every atom is joined to just three

❶ Examiner's tips

- Graphite is unusual because layers of atoms can slide over one another.
- Buckminster fullerene is also called a buckyball.
- Buckyballs and nanotubes are very strong and can conduct.
- Ordinary ice has the same structure as graphite.

Can you answer these questions?

1. What is the name given to the structures of diamond and graphite?
2. Why does graphite make a mark when rubbed on paper?
3. Why can't diamond conduct electricity?
4. How many covalent bonds does each carbon atom in a buckyball form?

Look on the CD for more exam practice questions

Did you know?

- You can change buckyballs into diamond using a very high pressure.

Models and medicine

Have you ever wondered?

If homeopathy works, why don't scientists believe it?

Key facts

- We can have different models of the same chemical.
- The chemicals in our bodies are very complex and many have complicated 3-D shapes.
- Chemists make 3-D models of new drugs on a computer to test how they will react with our body's chemicals.
- Before scientists test new drugs on animals, they test them in a laboratory on tissue cultures.
- Healthy volunteers test drugs for side effects before they are tested on patients.
- Conventional medicine is based on scientific method.
- Homeopathic medicines are very dilute and are based on 'like cures like'.
- Many chemists think that homeopathic medicines 'work' because the patient expects them to work – the placebo effect.

Definitions

- **homeopathic**
  A form of 'alternative' medicine based on 'like cures like' principle using very dilute forms of natural materials.

Look on the CD for more exam practice questions

❶ Examiner's tips

- Scientific method is based on observation, makes testable predictions and is supported by evidence.
- Homeopathy has no reliable experimental evidence to support it.
- Conventional medicine has a great deal of evidence to support it.

Can you answer these questions?

1. How do chemists test new medicines?
2. How are homeopathic medicines tested?
3. Why don't scientists believe that homeopathic medicines work?
4. What is the placebo effect?

Did you know?

- 11 days after inventing aspirin, Felix Hoffmann developed heroin as a pain killer.

How fast? How furious?

1 Making and breaking bonds

Have you ever wondered?

Why do some chemicals explode when you mix them?

Key facts

- Chemical bonds must be broken for a reaction to occur.
- **Collision theory** says reactions can only occur when the particles collide with enough energy.
- After this, the particles can reform as new chemicals making new bonds.
- Breaking bonds requires energy (endothermic), making bonds releases energy (exothermic).
- *All* reactions take in energy to break the bonds and release energy when making new bonds.
- An **endothermic reaction** takes in more energy than it releases.
- **Exothermic reactions** may need energy to start them, but they release even more energy and the temperature goes up, for example, burning.
- Endothermic reactions always need energy to start them and the temperature goes down, for example, adding water to ammonium nitrate.

Definitions

- **collision theory** The theory of chemical reactions that describes how particles must collide with enough energy to react.
- **endothermic reaction** A reaction that takes in heat energy from the surroundings.
- **exothermic reaction** A reaction that gives out heat energy to the surroundings.
- **rate of reaction** The speed at which a chemical reaction progresses.

❶ Examiner's tips

- Some reactions are so slow that it is difficult to see if they are exothermic or endothermic.
- The **rate of reaction** is a measure of how fast the reaction occurs.

Can you answer these questions?

1. 'Endo' means inside. What does 'exo' mean?
2. Why does breaking chemical bonds need energy?
3. Photosynthesis needs light energy to start the reaction. What type of energy is needed to start methane gas burning?

Did you know?

- All life on earth depends on an endothermic reaction, photosynthesis.

Look on the CD for more exam practice questions

② Concentration and surface area

Have you ever wondered?

Why do chips cook faster than roast potatoes?

Key facts

- When the reactant particles collide, reactions can take place.
- The reaction will only start if enough energy is available to break the bonds in the particles.
- Increasing the **concentration** increases the chance of the particles colliding and so the reaction is faster.
- Using smaller pieces of a solid reactant increases the **surface area**.
- The particles of a liquid reactant have more chance of colliding with the solid when the surface area is larger. This makes the reaction faster.
- Increasing the **pressure** of a gaseous reactant is the same as increasing its concentration and makes the reaction go faster.
- Increasing the frequency and the energy of collisions will increase the rate of reaction.

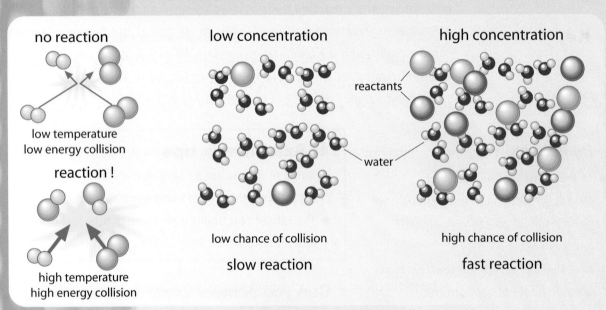

Definitions

- **concentration** The amount of a substance in a given volume of solution.
- **pressure** The force exerted per unit area (e.g. N/m^2).
- **surface area** The surface of a solid that is available for chemical reactions.

ⓘ Examiner's tips

- The rate of a reaction is calculated by
  $$\frac{1}{\text{time taken for the reaction}}.$$
- A powdered solid has a very large surface area.
- The speed of a reaction does not change how much product is formed at the end.

Look on the CD for more exam practice questions

Can you answer these questions?

1. What happens to the time a reaction takes when you
   (a) reduce the concentration of the reactant
   (b) make the lumps of a solid reactant larger?
2. If you give the particles more energy, will the reaction rate be
   A the same   B smaller   C greater?
3. How can you make two gases react faster while keeping their temperature constant?
4. What must happen to the particles for a reaction to occur?

Did you know?

- Each of our lungs has a surface area about the same size as the floor area of an average living room (just under 19 m^2).

3 Temperature and catalysts

Key facts

- Activation energy is needed to break bonds and start reactions.
- Increasing the **temperature** increases the rate of reaction by increasing the number of particles with enough energy to react.
- For many room temperature reactions, increasing the temperature by 10 °C doubles the rate of reaction.
- **Catalysts** speed up reactions but are chemically unchanged at the end of the reaction.
- **Enzymes** are biological catalysts made of protein which have complex shapes.
- Most enzymes work best at body temperatures and are specific to one reaction.
- Many reactions in our body are very slow so enzymes are essential to keep our body working well.

Definitions

- **catalyst** A substance that speeds up a chemical reaction without being used up.
- **enzyme** A biological catalyst.
- **temperature** A scale for measuring how 'hot' or 'cold' something is, usually measured in degrees Celsius (°C).

❶ Examiner's tips

- Many transition metals (and their compounds) are catalysts.
- Effective digestion of food relies on enzymes.
- Enzymes can be killed or denatured at a high temperature.

Look on the CD for more exam practice questions

Can you answer these questions?

1. How do catalysts affect the speed of a reaction?
2. Why does increasing the temperature increase the speed of the reaction?
3. What happens to the mass of a catalyst at the end of a reaction?
4. What happens to the speed of a reaction if the temperature decreases from 20 °C to 10 °C?

Did you know?

- Most of the enzymes originally used in 'biological' washing powders were found in bacteria adapted to live in hot springs.

④ Reaching a balance

Have you ever wondered?

Can chemical reactions be undone?

Key facts

- Some reactions are **reversible**; they are shown with this ⇌.
- If the conditions are changed the reaction can go backwards.
- In a closed system, the reaction reaches a balance or **equilibrium** with both reactants and products present.
- There is a **dynamic equilibrium** with both the forward and the backward reactions occurring at the same time.
- Changing the conditions changes the equilibrium position and the proportions of reactants and products present at equilibrium.
- A catalyst does not change the equilibrium position.
- When one (or more) of the chemical(s) is a gas, increasing the pressure favours the side of equation with the lowest number of gas molecules.

Type of reaction	Examples	Increasing the temperature	Increasing concentration of reactant
endothermic	thermal decomposition $CaCO_{3(s)} \rightleftharpoons CaO_{(s)} + CO_{2(g)}$	more product, less reactant	more product
exothermic	$H_{2(g)} + Cl_{2(g)} \rightleftharpoons 2HCl_{(g)}$ $3H_{2(g)} + N_{2(g)} \rightleftharpoons 2NH_{3(g)}$	less product	more product

Definitions

- **equilibrium**
  A balance point.
- **dynamic equilibrium**
  The equilibrium point in a reversible reaction where the rates of the forward and backward reactions are the same, so the proportions of different substances remain constant.
- **reversible**
  A chemical reaction that can be made to work in either direction.

❶ Examiner's tips

- Reactants are on the left hand side of the $\rightleftharpoons$.
- Take care when counting numbers of molecules of gas.
- The yield is the amount of product formed compared with the amount formed when the reaction goes to completion.

Can you answer these questions?

1. On which side of the equation do you write the products?
2. What effect has a catalyst on the rate and equilibrium position of a reaction?
3. What happens to the equilibrium yield of an exothermic reaction when you decrease the temperature?
4. What happens to the equilibrium yield of an endothermic reaction when you decrease the concentration of a reactant?

Look on the CD for more exam practice questions

Did you know?

- Many of our indicators (like phenolphthalein) use a reversible reaction to change colour in acids and alkalis.

⑤ Practically speaking

Key facts

- Data-loggers use sensors to measure physical quantities like mass, temperature and pH.
- Data-loggers can take measurements very quickly or over a long time.
- Measurements can be shown in tables and graphs on a computer.
- Data-loggers can be used in remote or dangerous places.
- The conditions of a reaction can be controlled by computers and data loggers.
- They are used in the industrial production of ammonia (**Haber process**).
- The reaction for ammonia production is $3H_{2(g)} + N_{2(g)} \rightleftharpoons 2NH_{3(g)}$.
  - The forward reaction is exothermic and reduces the number of gas molecules.
  - Increasing the pressure and reducing the temperature forms more ammonia.
  - The reaction is slow because nitrogen is very stable so iron is used as a catalyst.
  - The reaction is most economic when a lower yield is formed in a shorter time instead of a higher yield in a longer time.

Definitions

- **Haber process**
  The industrial process used to convert hydrogen and nitrogen into ammonia.

❶ Examiner's tips

- The ammonia produced in the Haber process is removed by cooling it to a liquid. The unreacted gases are recycled.
- The economic conditions are 200–300 atmospheres pressure and 400–450 °C.
- Ammonia is used to make fertilisers, explosives, window cleaning solutions, rocket fuel, and even cigarettes.

Look on the CD for more exam practice questions

Can you answer these questions?

1. State two examples of where using a data-logger is beneficial.
2. How can the data be displayed?
3. Explain why the ammonia produced in the Haber process is liquefied.

Did you know?

- 109 000 000 tonnes of ammonia was produced worldwide in 2004.

⑥ Fertilisers: artificial or organic?

Have you ever wondered?

How did the production of ammonia allow more of the world's population to be fed?

Key facts

- Ammonia is used to make many artificial **fertilisers**, for example, ammonium nitrate.
- Artificial fertilisers contain nitrogen, potassium or phosphorus which plants need for healthy growth.
- Ammonium nitrate contains 35% nitrogen and is soluble so plants can absorb it easily and quickly.
- Organic fertilisers such as manure, crushed bone and blood release nitrogen much more slowly.
- Overuse of any fertiliser can be uneconomic and cause pollution of rivers.
- Nitrates from fertilisers can cause eutrophication in rivers and may cause health problems.
- Some people prefer organic fertilisers as they believe these are better for the environment, biodiversity and soil structure.
- Organic farmers work harder and longer for often a lower yield.

Definitions

- **fertiliser**
  Something which provides the essential minerals that plants need to grow.

Look on the CD for more exam practice questions

❶ Examiner's tips

- Babies are most at risk from nitrates in drinking water.
- Eutrophication means that algae on the surface grow very well but plants and wildlife have insufficient oxygen to survive.

Can you answer these questions?

1. State two advantages each of artificial and organic fertilisers.
2. What are the main minerals needed by plants for healthy growth?
3. What does biodiversity mean?

Did you know?

- Powdered limestone and fish emulsion are made in factories, but are classified as organic fertilisers.

As fast as you can!

1 Speed and velocity

Have you ever wondered?

What is the difference between speed and velocity?

Key facts

- Distance is a measure of how far apart objects or places are.
- Distance in a particular direction is called displacement.
- **Speed** is a measure of how far an object moves in a given time.
- **Velocity** is the speed of an object in a particular direction.
- Velocity is a **vector** – a quantity with both **magnitude** (size) and direction.
- Average velocity (*v*), displacement (*s*) and time (*t*) are related by the equation:

$$\text{average velocity} = \frac{\text{displacement}}{\text{time}} \qquad v = \frac{s}{t}$$

Definitions

- **magnitude** A measure of how big something is.
- **speed** A measure of the distance an object travels in a given time. Usually measured in metres per second (m/s).
- **vector** A quantity that has a size and direction. Force and velocity are examples of vectors. Speed, mass and volume are *not* vectors.
- **velocity** The speed of an object in a particular direction. Usually measured in metres per second (m/s).

Look on the CD for more exam practice questions

❶ Examiner's tips

- Divide the distance by the time to get the speed.
- Divide the displacement by the time to get the velocity.
- Speed and velocity have the same unit. They are both measured in m/s.
- Remember that **velocity** is a **vector**.

Can you answer these questions?

1. What is the unit for speed?
2. What is the difference between speed and velocity?
3. A racing car moves 240 metres along a straight part of the track in 4 seconds. What is the velocity of the racing car?
4. A football is kicked away from the goal and the players pass the ball between them. After 50 seconds the ball is kicked into the other goal 100 metres away. While it was being passed between the players the ball actually moved 250 metres.
   (a) What was the average velocity of the ball between the two goals?
   (b) What was the average speed of the ball during the first 50 seconds?

Did you know?

- The fastest possible speed is the speed of light, which is 300 000 000 m/s. At that speed, you could go more than seven times around the Earth in a second.

② Acceleration

Have you ever wondered?

Could you manage the acceleration to be a good Formula 1 driver?

Key facts

- **Acceleration** is a measure of how fast velocity changes.
- When velocity changes, its size or its direction can change.
- Acceleration (a), velocity change ($v - u$) and time (t) are related by the equation:

$$\text{acceleration} = \frac{\text{change in velocity}}{\text{time}} \qquad a = \frac{v - u}{t}$$

- This relationship can be shown on a graph of velocity against time. The acceleration is shown by the **gradient** of the graph.
- Acceleration is measured in metres per second each second (or m/s²).

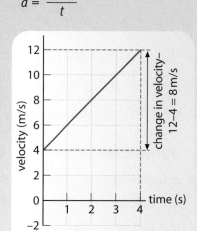

Acceleration = 8/4 = 2 m/s²

Definitions

- **acceleration**
  A measure of how quickly the velocity of an object is changing (measured in metres per second per second (m/s²)).

- **gradient**
  A measurement of the steepness of the slope of a graph. The steeper the graph, the higher the gradient.

Look on the CD for more exam practice questions

❶ Examiner's tips

- You should be able to sketch velocity–time graphs.
- Acceleration can be positive (speeding up) or negative (slowing down).
- The steeper the gradient, the bigger the acceleration.
- Magnitude just means size.

Can you answer these questions?

1. What is a unit for acceleration?
2. In which two ways can a velocity change?
3. A high speed train accelerates to 70 m/s from 0 m/s in a time of 350 s.
   (a) What is the acceleration of the train?
   (b) Why does a train driver usually choose to accelerate so gently?
4. When a space shuttle is about to re-enter the atmosphere, it is slowed down so that the velocity changes from 8 km/s to 7 km/s in 200 s.
   (a) Sketch a velocity–time graph to show the change.
   (b) Calculate the space shuttle's acceleration.

Did you know?

- Some roller coasters can reach speeds of 160 km/h within 7 seconds. They accelerate faster than most cars.

3 Force, mass and acceleration

Have you ever wondered?

How much you know about the laws of physics if you skate, snowboard or play flight simulators?

Key facts

- The size of the **resultant force** is the sum of all the forces acting in a particular direction.
- Forces come in pairs. There will be always be a **reaction** to any **action**.
- The action and the reaction are the same size, but they have opposite directions.
- A resistive force always acts in the opposite direction to any movement.
- The forces on an object can be shown as arrows on a diagram.
- Force (*F*), mass (*m*) and acceleration (*a*) are related by the equation:

  force = mass × acceleration $F = m\,a$

Definitions

- **action** In physics, one of a pair of forces. The reaction force acts in the opposite direction.
- **reaction** In physics, one of a pair of forces. This acts in the opposite direction to the action force.
- **resultant force** The total force that results from two or more forces acting on a single object. It is found by adding the forces together, taking into account their direction.

❶ Examiner's tips

- The unit for force is the newton (N).
- Forces acting in one direction are regarded as positive and forces in the opposite direction as negative.
- Multiplying the mass by the acceleration will give the resultant force.
- Another word for resistance is drag.

Can you answer these questions?

1. When you are sitting still, which two forces act vertically on you?
2. Donna is driving along the motorway. Sketch a diagram to show the vertical and horizontal forces on her car.
3. An aeroplane has a mass of 300 000 kg and is accelerating along the runway at 3 m/s².
   (a) What is the resultant force on the aeroplane?
   (b) If the forward force from the engines is 1 000 000 N, what is the size and direction of the resistance?

Did you know?

- A force of one newton (1 N) is about the same as the weight of a small apple.

Look on the CD for more exam practice questions

④ Falling

Have you ever wondered?

Do the experiences of bungee jumping, parachuting and free-fall all feel the same?

Key facts

The forces on a sky diver.

- If there is no resultant force on an object it will either stay still or move with constant velocity.
- Constant velocity means that the speed and the direction stay the same.
- An object falling in air feels two forces: the force of gravity (**weight**) and a resistive force (air **resistance**).
- If the weight is bigger than the air resistance then the object will accelerate downwards.
- As a falling object picks up speed, the air resistance increases.
- As the air resistance increases, the resultant force decreases.
- When an object reaches **terminal velocity**, the air resistance and the weight are equal and opposite.

Definitions

- **resistance** In physics, a force that acts in the opposite direction of motion. Friction is an example of a resistance force.
- **terminal velocity** A constant, maximum velocity reached by falling objects. This happens when the weight downwards is equal to the air resistance upwards.
- **weight** The force pulling an object downwards. It depends on the mass of the object and the strength of gravity.

❶ Examiner's tips

- Weight is the pull of gravity. It makes objects fall towards the ground.
- If an object is not moving, then there is no air resistance.
- If there is no resultant force on an object, there can be no acceleration.
- If there is no acceleration then velocity cannot change.

Can you answer these questions?

1. Explain what is meant by constant velocity.
2. A bus is not accelerating. What does this tell you about the resultant force on the bus?
3. Sharon weighs 600 N. She is bungee jumping. As she falls, the upward force from the elastic is 200 N and increasing.
   (a) What is the resultant force on Sharon?
   (b) What will happen to Sharon's velocity and acceleration?
4. People weigh less on the Moon, but there is no air. Explain why it would be dangerous for astronauts to try sky diving on the Moon.

Look on the CD for more exam practice questions

Did you know?

- A vertical wind tunnel helps sky divers to practise safely indoors. Air rushing upwards through a grill in the floor supports their weight and they stay near the ground.

⑤ Stopping safely

Have you ever wondered?

Which make of car saves most lives in a crash?

Key facts

- The faster a car is moving, the longer the **stopping distance** that it needs.
- When the road is wet or slippery, stopping distances are longer.
- Stopping distance increases when a driver's reaction time increases.
- **Momentum**, mass and velocity are related by the equation:

  momentum = mass × velocity

- Safety features such as seatbelts, airbags and crumple zones are designed to absorb a passenger's momentum gradually in an accident.
- If the momentum changes more slowly then the force on the passenger is less and their chance of injury is reduced.

Definitions

- **momentum**
  A quantity describing the movement of an object. Calculated by multiplying the mass by the velocity.
- **stopping distance**
  The distance a car travels between when the driver sees something and when the car stops. Found by adding thinking distance and braking distance.

❶ Examiner's tips

- The unit for momentum is kilogram metres per second (kg m/s).
- Stopping distance = thinking distance + braking distance.
- Tiredness, alcohol and drugs can all increase a driver's reaction time.
- If velocity changes more slowly, then the momentum also changes more slowly.

Can you answer these questions?

1. What factors can increase the stopping distance of a car?
2. Why does the driver's thinking time affect the stopping distance?
3. The mass of a car is 1500 kg and its velocity is 40 m/s. What is the car's momentum?
4. Jim sells glass light bulbs by mail order. Explain why it is a good idea for him to pack the light bulbs in bubble wrap before they are sent in the post.

Did you know?

- Most people who buy a new car ask about the safety features for passengers before choosing the model. Far fewer people seem to be worried about how dangerous their car might be for pedestrians.

Look on the CD for more exam practice questions

6 How dangerous?

Have you ever wondered?

What is the chance of you being injured in a high-speed outdoor activity?

Key facts

- Sometimes computers are better at collecting data than people.
- Computer data, such as data about **collisions**, can be entered into a spreadsheet and used to model a situation.
- Risk can be expressed as a percentage – how many times in a hundred something will happen.
- A 100% risk means that something will always happen; a 0% risk will never happen.
- A person's experience can reduce a risk, or make a risk more acceptable to them.
- People are more likely to do something risky if it is their own choice.

Definitions

- **collision** When two or more objects come into contact with each other.

❶ Examiner's tips

- Some people find the idea of danger thrilling, so they may choose to take unnecessary risks.
- Computer modelling allows scientists to try out 'what if' situations without the risks of the real world.

Look on the CD for more exam practice questions

Can you answer these questions?

1. Explain why pilots use a computer flight simulator instead of flying a real aeroplane when they are practising emergency landings.
2. Why do lots of people go skiing even though there is a significant risk of serious injury?
3. If ten people choose to jump across a wide stream, two of them will fall in. What is the risk of getting wet feet when crossing the stream?
4. Explain why a trainee at a building site may be more likely to be injured than an experienced worker.

Did you know?

- The *Titanic* was thought to have been designed to withstand most types of accident, so the passengers felt very safe because they believed the risk of the ship sinking was so small. An unlucky sequence of events caused the *Titanic* to sink.

Roller coasters and relativity

1 Work, work, work

Have you ever wondered?

How do you work out how much work you do?

Key facts

- **Work done** is equal to the energy transferred.
- Work done, **force** and **distance** are related by the equation:

  Work done = force × distance moved in the direction of the force

  $$W = F \times s$$

- The force and the distance are in the same direction.
- The greater the force, the greater the amount of work done.
- The further the distance, the greater the amount of work done.

Definitions

- **distance** A measure of how far apart objects or places are, measured in metres (m).
- **force** An action on an object that makes it accelerate, decelerate or change shape, measured in newtons (N).
- **work done** The energy transferred by a force on a moving object, measured in joules (J).

❶ Examiner's tips

- Work is a form of energy, so it is measured in joules (J).
- When work is done against the force of gravity, the distance moved is the same as the change in height.

Can you answer these questions?

1. What is the unit for work?
2. In what direction should you measure the distance moved when calculating the work done?
3. Anne pushes her lawnmower with a force of 25 N. While she is cutting the grass, the lawnmower moves forward 150 m. How much work does Anne do?
4. Tom is lifting some packets of sugar onto a shelf. There are 30 packets and each weighs 10 N. He lifts them 1.5 m from the ground. How much energy is transferred when he lifts all the packets?

Did you know?

- When the ancient Egyptians constructed the great Pyramid at Giza, the builders needed to do more than 2 000 000 000 000 joules (2 terajoules) of work to lift the stones up into position.

Look on the CD for more exam practice questions

2 Power and electrical energy

Have you ever wondered?

Where does the power come from to make a theme park ride accelerate faster than a space shuttle?

Key facts

- The more powerful something is, the faster it can transfer energy.
- The equation for calculating **power** is:

  power = work done ÷ time taken $P = W \div t$
- Power is a number of watts (W) or kilowatts (kW).
- The equation for calculating **electrical energy** is:

  electrical energy = **voltage** × **current** × time $E = V \times I \times t$
- Electrical energy is a number of joules (J) or kilojoules (kJ).

Definitions

- **current** The flow of electricity around a circuit, measured in amps (A) or milliamps (mA).
- **electrical energy** The energy made available by a current. Measured in joules (J).
- **power** A measure of how quickly energy is transferred, measured in watts (W) or kilowatts (kW).
- **voltage** The difference in electrical energy between two points that causes a current, measured in volts (V). It is sometimes called the potential difference.

❶ Examiner's tips

- Electrical energy is the same as electrical power × time.
- Increasing any one of the voltage, the current or the time will increase the amount of energy transferred.
- Electrical energy can also be measured in kWh.

Can you answer these questions?

1. What is a watt?
2. A linear motor transfers 300 000 J of energy to a roller coaster car in 4 seconds. What is the power of the motor?
3. The motor in a paper shredder runs for 8 seconds. The voltage is 230 V and the current is 1.8 A. How much electrical energy is transferred?
4. How much electrical energy does a 150 W television transfer during a $\frac{1}{2}$ hour TV programme?

Did you know?

- An ordinary 60 W light bulb is designed to last at least 2500 hours before it burns out.

Look on the CD for more exam practice questions

③ Potential energy and kinetic energy

Have you ever wondered?

If you could design a roller coaster ride, what would it look like?

Key facts

- The acceleration of free-fall is 9.8 m/s^2.
- The acceleration of free-fall is usually written as g.
- The formula for calculating **gravitational potential energy** transferred is:

    potential energy transferred = **mass** × acceleration of free-fall × change in height

    $$GPE = m \times g \times h$$
- The formula for calculating **kinetic energy** is:

    kinetic energy = $\frac{1}{2}$ × mass × (**velocity**)^2

    $$KE = \frac{1}{2}mv^2$$

Definitions

- **gravitational potential energy** The energy involved in moving anything against the force of gravity, such as lifting an object. It depends upon the mass of the object, the distance moved and the gravitational field strength. Measured in joules (J).
- **kinetic energy** The energy of a moving object, measured in joules (J). It depends upon the mass of the object and the velocity at which it is travelling.
- **mass** The amount of matter in an object, measured in kilograms (kg).
- **velocity** The speed of an object in a particular direction. Usually measured in metres per second (m/s).

Look on the CD for more exam practice questions

❶ Examiner's tips

- g tells you how fast objects will accelerate when they fall.
- Both GPE and KE are measured in joules (J).
- Kinetic energy increases quickly when speed increases.

Can you answer these questions?

1. What is the unit for kinetic energy?
2. A bird flies from the ground to the top of a 15 m tree. The mass of the bird is 0.1 kg and $g = 9.8$ m/s^2. How much gravitational potential energy is transferred?
3. A tennis ball has a mass of 0.056 kg and is moving at 50 m/s. How much kinetic energy does the tennis ball have?
4. Which of these has more kinetic energy:
    (a) a 10 000 kg bus moving at 12 m/s,
    (b) a 400 kg motorbike moving at 60 m/s?

Did you know?

- The finish of an Olympic downhill ski race is about 1000 m below the start. The fastest skiers reach speeds of 35 m/s.

How roller coasters keep moving

Have you ever wondered?

How do you make the biggest water splash?

Key facts

- Energy cannot be created or destroyed. This is the law of **conservation of energy**.
- Energy can be converted from one form to another.
- When an object falls, gravitational potential energy is transferred into kinetic energy.
- Usually, roller coaster cars are released from the top of a hill.
- The cars accelerate as they coast down the slope.
- The cars follow a track that runs downhill, uphill and round curves.
- The passengers experience forces and **acceleration** changes when the cars change direction and **speed**.

Definitions

- **acceleration** A measure of how quickly the velocity of an object is changing (measured in metres per second per second (m/s^2)).
- **conservation of energy** A law that states that energy can be converted from one form to another but cannot be created or destroyed.
- **speed** A measure of the distance an object travels in a given time. Usually measured in metres per second (m/s).

❶ Examiner's tips

- Most roller coasters are designed to transfer *GPE* into *KE*.
- Sometimes roller coaster cars are moved by a motor at the start. Electrical energy transfers to *KE*.
- Sudden tight corners and turning upside down can cause big acceleration changes for the passengers.
- Usually some of the energy transferred ends up as thermal energy (heat).

Can you answer these questions?

1. Name three forms of energy.
2. A roller coaster starts at the top of a hill, rolls down and is stopped by its brakes. Outline the energy changes that occur.
3. Using the words *accelerate*, *force*, *energy* and *velocity*, briefly explain the physics involved when an electric motor starts a roller coaster car moving along a flat track.
4. Why do you think people enjoy riding on roller coasters?

Did you know?

- Some roller coasters feature an Immelmann loop – a half loop and a half roll that sends you travelling back in the opposite direction. This manoeuvre was invented by a pilot who flew aircraft more than ninety years ago.

 Look on the CD for more exam practice questions

⑤ Going round in circles

Have you ever wondered?

When you ride on a roller coaster, what is it that drives you round the bend?

Key facts

- When an object moves in a circle, the direction of its velocity keeps changing.
- If its velocity is changing, then the object must be **accelerating**.
- If the object is accelerating, then there must be a **resultant force** on it.
- When an object moves in a circle, the force on it is inwards, towards the centre.

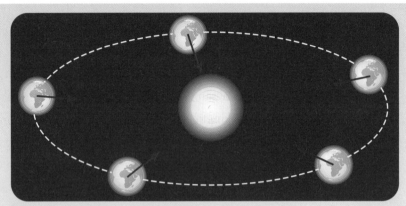

The force acts towards the centre.

Definitions

- **acceleration** A measure of how quickly the velocity of an object is changing (measured in metres per second per second m/s^2)).
- **constant speed** The movement of an object that covers the same distance every second, neither accelerating nor decelerating.
- **resultant force** The total force that results from two or more forces acting on a single object. It is found by adding the forces together, taking into account their direction.

❶ Examiner's tips

- If you move round a circle at a **constant speed**, the size of the acceleration also stays the same.
- The force of gravity (towards the centre of the Earth) keeps orbiting satellites moving in a circle.

Can you answer these questions?

1. A fly sits on the minute hand of a clock. The minute hand is turning slowly. Describe how the fly's speed and velocity change.
2. Wendy is riding on a roundabout. Her chair is moving in a circle. Draw a diagram to show the forces on Wendy.
3. A satellite is orbiting the Earth at constant speed. Explain why it is accelerating.
4. George feels weightless when he is turned upside down by the corkscrew-shaped track of a roller coaster. Draw a diagram to show the forces on George when he is upside down and moving in a circle.

Look on the CD for more exam practice questions

Did you know?

- When your washing machine is spin drying, the wet clothes are pressed with a force more than three times their own weight.

Einstein and relativity

Have you ever wondered?

How did Einstein come up with the most famous idea in physics, the **theory of relativity**?

Key facts

- Einstein used thought experiments rather than real measurements to develop his theories.
- Some things cannot be discovered just by studying data.
- Few scientists accepted Einstein's ideas when he first published them.
- Scientists rarely accept new ideas before there is proper evidence for them.
- Most scientists now believe that Einstein's theory of relativity is correct because it has been tested experimentally.
- Experiments have shown that Einstein was correct to say that mass can be turned into energy and that time slows down for objects which are moving.

Definitions

- **theory of relativity**
  A theory put forward by Albert Einstein that connects different areas of physics including mass, energy, gravity, movement, space and time.

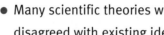
Look on the CD for more exam practice questions

❶ Examiner's tips

- Many scientific theories were not accepted at first, especially if they disagreed with existing ideas.
- Scientific method requires proper experimental proof before theories are accepted as fact.

Can you answer these questions?

1. What is a thought experiment?
2. Explain why most scientists did not accept Einstein's theory at first.
3. Explain why most scientists now do accept Einstein's theory.
4. In the 1980s a team of scientists announced that they had discovered a process called 'cold fusion', but other scientists were not able to repeat the experiment. Explain why most scientists do not accept that 'cold fusion' was discovered.

Did you know?

- Einstein was only sixteen when he worked out that the speed of light must always be the same, whether you are moving or not.

Putting radiation to use

1 Radioactivity: what and where from?

Have you ever wondered?

Radioactivity destroys cancers but does it leave a patient radioactive afterwards?

Key facts

- Radioactivity is concerned with radiation from the nucleus of atoms.
- There are three types of **ionising radiation**: alpha (α), beta (β) and gamma (γ).
- α-particles are the nuclei of helium atoms and, because they are relatively large, they produce great amounts of ionisation in a short distance and so do not penetrate far before losing their energy.
- β-particles are fast moving 'electrons' (from the nucleus) and can penetrate further before losing their energy by ionisation.
- γ-rays are pure energy. They are just like light, but have a very high frequency. They can penetrate great distances but produce very little ionisation in a given distance.
- α-particles are stopped by about 6 cm of air or a piece of paper. β-particles are stopped by 3 or 4 mm of aluminium. Some γ-rays can pass through many centimetres of lead.
- α- and β-particles and γ-rays are emitted from unstable nuclei in a random way.

Definitions

- **ionising radiation**
  Form of radiation that causes ionisation in atoms through which it passes – the atoms lose electrons from their outer shells and so become charged overall – they become ions.

✆ Examiner's tips

- Radiation which penetrates further is less strongly ionising.
- X-rays and γ-rays are indistinguishable when moving.
- X-rays and γ-rays have similar properties but differ in the way they are produced.
- The Earth's atmosphere absorbs many of the radiations from space.

Can you answer these questions?

1. Which is the most penetrating form of radiation?
2. Which radiation is most ionising in a short distance?
3. Which radiation is most like visible light?
4. Complete the table.

name of radiation	symbol of ray	type of charge	penetrating power	ionising power
alpha			low	
beta		negative		medium
	γ			

Look on
the CD
for more
exam
practice
questions

Did you know?

- The thick concrete tomb surrounding the damaged nuclear reactor at Chernobyl is to be replaced by a steel shell of mass 20 000 000 kg.

② Structure of an atom

Have you ever wondered?

What is an atom like?

Key facts

- Atoms consist of protons, neutrons and electrons.
- In the middle of the atom is a nucleus, like a nut in its shell.
- The electrons are in orbit around this central nucleus.
- Nuclei contain protons and neutrons.
- All nuclei of the same element contain the same number of protons.
- If nuclei of the same element contain different numbers of neutrons they are called **isotopes**.
- Isotopes of an element have the same **atomic (proton) number** but different **mass (nucleon) numbers**.

Definitions

- **atomic (proton) number** The number of protons present in the nucleus of all atoms of one particular element.
- **isotope** Atoms of an element with the same number of protons and electrons but different numbers of neutrons
- **mass (nucleon) number** The combined total number of neutrons and protons in the nucleus of one particular isotope of an element. Also called nucleon number.

❶ Examiner's tips

- Nuclei are identified by two numbers written near the symbol for the element like this: $^{3}_{2}\text{He}$
- The 2 is the number of protons (the atomic (proton) number) which is the same for all helium nuclei.
- The 3 is the total number of protons PLUS neutrons. It is the mass (nucleon) number.
- The number of neutrons is thus 3 − 2 = 1.
- In a nuclear equation the sum of the top numbers on each side of the equation is equal and so is the sum of the bottom numbers on each side.

$$^{238}_{92}\text{U} \rightarrow {}^{234}_{90}\text{Th} + {}^{4}_{2}\alpha$$

Can you answer these questions?

1. The diagram shows the protons and neutrons in a lithium nucleus.
   Complete the symbol for the lithium nucleus.

   $\square \atop \square$ Li

2. Here is a nuclear equation for two elements X and Y.

   $$^2_1 X + ^2_\square X \rightarrow ^\square_\square Y$$

   (a) Complete the equation.

   (b) How many protons are there in each X?

   (c) How many neutrons are there in Y?

   (d) What is the mass (nucleon) number of Y?

3. Which of these are isotopes of hydrogen? $^3_1 Z$ $^2_2 Z$ $^2_1 Z$

Did you know?

- The nucleus was discovered because alpha particles can pass through very thin gold foil. This showed that most of an atom is empty space. Some, however, bounced back, showing the positive charge and that most of the mass is concentrated in a very small volume.

③ Radioactivity in action

Have you ever wondered?

Why do some people wear radioactive watches that shine in the dark?

Key facts

- Alpha particle emitters are used in fire (smoke) alarms as they are absorbed easily by air/smoke.
- Beta particles are absorbed by different thicknesses of metals and so help to monitor thickness.
- Gamma rays can be used in the **sterilisation** of equipment in hospitals. They kill bacteria but are no longer dangerous after being absorbed.
- Gamma rays help doctors diagnose problems because radioactive materials can be traced inside the body.
- Gamma rays treat cancer by killing cells inside the body.

Definitions

- **sterilisation** Process where bacteria and viruses on an object are destroyed. Sterilisation can be carried out using radioactive sources.

❶ Examiner's tips

- The uses of the different radiations depend on their properties.
- If you are asked to choose the best radiation to use for a job, think about the properties of the radiations.
- The main differences are in penetration/ionisation and the effect of charges and magnetic fields on them. Also think about the half-life (see next section) of the source.

Look on the CD for more exam practice questions

Can you answer these questions?

1. What gas will be produced when alpha particles are stopped?

2. The diagram shows how β-particles are used to monitor whether packets of soap powder are full.

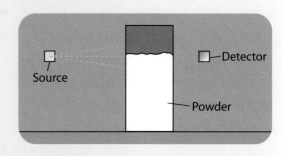

Source · · · □—Detector · Powder

   (a) Why are alpha particles not used?

   (b) Why are gamma rays not used?

   (c) What will happen to the reading from the detector if the level of the powder is below what it should be?

Did you know?

- Food can be made to last longer by shining ionising radiation on to it. It does not change the taste.

④ Changes in activity with time

Have you ever wondered?

How do we know things such as 'Woolly mammoths died out 10 000 years ago', which is before humans learned to write?

Key facts

- The rate of decay of a radioactive material depends on the number of atoms/molecules left to decay. It is a **random process**.
- The fewer particles left, the smaller the chance of decay.
- The **activity** (measured in becquerels) is the number of particles decaying in a given time.
- The activity reduces as time passes according to the graph shown.

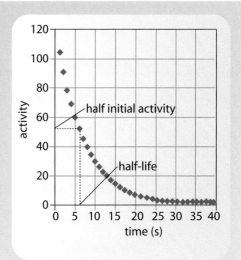

- The **half-life** of a material is the time for the original mass of material to decay to half that mass or for the activity to fall to half its initial value
- Scientists can date historical objects by comparing the activity of a sample now with known activities in the past.

Definitions

- **activity** The number of emissions of radiation from a sample in a given time. Sometimes this is given as counts per minute or, more correctly, as becquerels (Bq).
- **half-life** A measure of how quickly some radioactive substances decay. It is the average time for half of the atoms originally present to have decayed.
- **random process** Process such as radioactive decay in which the timing of the next event cannot be predicted.

❶ Examiner's tips

- Measurement of the age of an object is made uncertain, for example, by:
  - experimental error
  - assuming that cosmic rays and climate have stayed constant
  - burning fossil fuels and testing atomic bombs.
- Computers are used to analyse decays because:
  - they produce graphs more accurately and quickly
  - data-loggers can be used and they plot data as it is obtained
  - some half-lives need very short times to be measured.
- Radioactive carbon-14 can be used to date samples which contained living matter.
- Rocks can be dated by comparing the proportion of radioactive isotopes in them.

Look on the CD for more exam practice questions

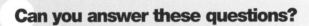

Can you answer these questions?

This graph shows the activity of a sample from a tree.

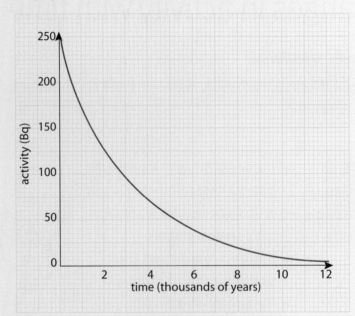

1. What is the activity at a time of 2000 years?
2. At what time is the activity 150 Bq?
3. What is the half-life of the material?

Did you know?

- The half-life of U-238 is about 4500 million years and is almost the same as the age of the Earth. In contrast, the half-lives of some nuclei are less than 10^{-21} s and decay almost as soon as they are formed!

⑤ Background radiation

Have you ever wondered?

What makes the 'Northern lights' the most colourful sight on Earth?

Key facts

- There is radiation around us all the time. This is **background radiation.**
- Living things contain radioactive materials and so produce radiation.
- Some rocks are radioactive.
- **Radon gas** is a radioactive gas which can be trapped in rocks or under house floors.
- We receive radiation from the Sun but also from space.
- The Earth's magnetic field and atmosphere protect us by directing and absorbing cosmic rays and changing the energy into light energy to give the northern (and southern) lights.

Definitions

- **background radiation**
  Radiation that is all around us all the time from a number of sources. Some background radiation is naturally occurring, while some has its origins in human activities.
- **radon gas**
  Naturally occurring, radioactive gas that is emitted from rocks underground.

Look on the CD for more exam practice questions

❶ Examiner's tips

- The background count must be allowed for in all experimental readings.
- The background count must be taken with all apparatus, except the source, set up at the site of the experiment.
- Radon is a gas which we breathe into our bodies. Different isotopes emit alpha and beta particles which kill or mutate cells there.

Can you answer these questions?

1. This pie chart shows the main sources of background radiation.

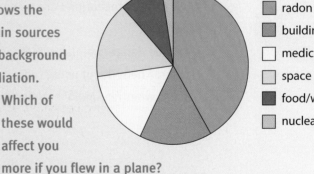

- radon
- buildings/soil
- medicine
- space (cosmic rays)
- food/water
- nuclear industry

   (a) Which of these would affect you more if you flew in a plane?

   (b) Which two of these are not natural radiations?

2. What causes the Northern Lights (or Aurora Borealis)?

Did you know?

- Thousands of rays from space pass through you every minute, without noticeably affecting you.

Dangers and risks

Have you ever wondered?

Irradiating food makes it last longer, so why won't the supermarkets sell food treated in this way? Could a low dose of radioactivity actually be good for you?

Key facts

- Alpha particles are dangerous inside the body because they lose their energy by ionising parts of the body. They don't, however, pass through the skin.
- If DNA is damaged, **mutations** can occur. Mutations can be good or, more usually, bad and may affect future generations.
- Ionising radiations can kill cells. This can be harmful but some of the cells that are killed might be cancerous.
- Safety precautions in schools are there to restrict exposure of young people to radiation and prevent ingestion of material.

Definitions

- **mutation**
  Change that takes place in a living organism, often as a result of interaction with radiation.

❶ Examiner's tips

- With care, some uses of radioactivity might be worth the risk.
- You should think about the benefits as well as the risks of a particular application: smoke alarms are usually considered worth the risk but in other applications, the dangers may outweigh the benefits.
- Radioactive waste is difficult to dispose of because some isotopes have long half-lives.

Look on the CD for more exam practice questions

Can you answer these questions?

1. What safety precautions are taken when using radioactive sources in schools?
2. List *three* dangers of using radioactive materials.
3. List *three* benefits of using radioactivity.
4. Discuss whether smoke alarms which contain radioactivity should be used.

Did you know?

- Marie Curie was clever enough to be presented with two Nobel prizes but still died because she did not have the knowledge about radioactivity to take the basic safety precautions that we take now.

Power of the atom

① Fission and chain reactions

Key facts

- A few materials (such as uranium-235 and plutonium-239) split into two large parts (**daughter products**) when hit by a neutron (**fission**).
- The splitting also produces two or three more neutrons.
- Each of these neutrons may cause further fissions.
- This is a **chain reaction**.
- Not all the neutrons will cause further fission. Some may be absorbed by impurities, others escape through the surface.
- The daughter products of nuclear fission are radioactive.
- The daughter nuclei will be the start of a **decay series**.

Definitions

- **chain reaction** The sequence of reactions produced when a nuclear fission reaction triggers one or more new fissions.
- **daughter products** The two nuclei produced when a nucleus undergoes fission.
- **decay series** A sequence of radioactive isotopes and their radiation. When a radioactive isotope decays, it may form a new radioactive nucleus. This in turn decays into another nucleus. The series goes on until it reaches a stable nucleus.
- **fission** The reaction when the nucleus of a heavy atom splits into two smaller nuclei.

❶ Examiner's tips

- Because the fission products are radioactive, the waste from nuclear reactors has to be stored carefully.
- Each fission releases energy.
- If more than one neutron produces a further fission, the energy production increases very rapidly and an explosion can occur.

Can you answer these questions?

1. This diagram represents part of a chain reaction.

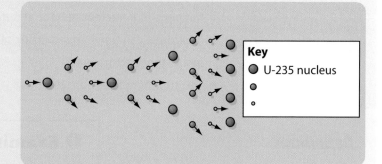

Key
- U-235 nucleus

(a) Complete the key.

(b) Describe what is happening in this reaction. (There are several steps to describe.)

Look on the CD for more exam practice questions

2. Ten dominoes are standing on end next to each other. When the end domino is knocked over it knocks the next, etc. Describe how this models a chain reaction.

3. Suppose the two neutrons from one fission each cause a further fission. These will release 4 neutrons which will in turn release 8 neutrons, and so on. How many stages of fission will be needed to produce 256 neutrons at one go?

Did you know?

- The idea of detecting a chain reaction occurred to a scientist as he walked across a road!

② Power stations

Have you ever wondered?

Should we switch to nuclear power to stop global warming because it doesn't produce greenhouse gases?

Key facts

- If *more than one* neutron from one fission causes a further fission (on average) the **thermal energy** release increases very rapidly and an *explosion* can occur.
- If *fewer than one* neutron causes a further fission, the reaction will *die out*.
- If the purity and size of the sample means that *exactly one* neutron (on average) causes a further fission, energy is produced at a *steady rate*. This happens in a **nuclear reactor** at a power station.
- Impurities can be changed artificially by raising or lowering control rods inside the reactor core.
- The control rods absorb neutrons.

Definitions

- **nuclear reactor** The part of a nuclear power station that holds the fuel rods and control rods. It is where controlled fission takes place to produce heat for generating electricity.
- **thermal energy** The energy associated with a hot body. Measured in joules (J).

❶ Examiner's tips

- Consider how improving the purity of the sample will affect the rate of reaction.
- Consider how decreasing the size of the sample will affect the rate of reaction.
- Waste from reactors must be stored safely for a long time. Burying it in a deep hole on a secure site seems to be the option most likely to be accepted.

Look on the CD for more exam practice questions

Can you answer these questions?

1. Explain what will happen to the rate of reaction if the average number of neutrons causing further fission is: (a) 0.7   (b) 1.2.
2. Explain the effect on the rate of reaction of lowering the control rods into the core.
3. Draw a diagram including neutrons and five U-235 nuclei only to represent the chain reaction occurring in a power station.

Did you know?

● Nature had 15 working, controlled nuclear reactors (caused by a peculiar combination of rock and water conditions and algae), at a place in Africa called Oklo, nearly 2 billion years ago.

③ Electrostatics

Have you ever wondered?

What should you do if you're in the countryside when lightning strikes?

Key facts

● Charged objects attract uncharged objects.
● Like charges repel (**repulsion**), opposite charges attract.
● An object can become charged by contact with a charged object.
● Objects can be charged by rubbing against another insulator or insulated object.
● Objects become charged or discharged by the transfer of electrons.
● Lightning is caused by charges which have built up in a cloud discharging to earth along the shortest path.

Definitions

● **electrostatics**
Effects created by electrical charges that do not move.
● **repulsion**
A force that pushes two objects apart.

❶ Examiner's tips

● The amount of positive charge left on a duster is equal to the amount of negative charge rubbed off onto a rod.
● Only insulated or insulating objects can be charged, because otherwise the objects will be earthed.
● In metallic conductors, it is the negative electrons which move.

Can you answer these questions?

1. What will happen when a positively charged object passes near a negatively charged object?
2. Why do electrons move rather than positively charged protons?
3. Why do electrons not escape from an atom easily?

Did you know?

I'm safe if I stay inside here!

Look on the CD for more exam practice questions

④ Uses and dangers of electrostatics

Have you ever wondered?

Is it magic or physics when your teacher creates lightning bolts and make objects levitate?

Key facts

- Fuel and pipe can become charged with an **electrostatic** charge as fuel passes through a pipe. Aeroplanes and fuel tankers (bowsers) are earthed during refuelling to prevent explosions due to sparks.
- When you walk across a nylon carpet, you can become charged. You then get a shock from a metal door handle.
- Particles can be removed from smoke if a charged wire is in a chimney.
- Plastic film is an insulator and becomes charged as it is pulled off a roll. This can be used to pick up dust and sweat left by fingerprints or to make an airtight seal around food.

Definitions

- **electrostatics**
  Effects created by electrical charges that do not move.
- **electric current**
  The movement of charge – electrons in a wire.

❶ Examiner's tips

- Workers in some electronics industries wear bracelets connected to earth to prevent them becoming charged.
- Static charges can move through conductors. The moving charges are then an **electric current**!

Can you answer these questions?

1. Use the idea of forces between charges to explain why it is an advantage to charge a bicycle frame positively when the paint coming from the sprayer is negatively charged.
2. The steps in the operation of a laser printer are given below. Only the first and last are in the correct order. Write a letter against the rest to show the correct order.

A The rotating drum is charged positively.

   This stronger charge pulls toner to the paper.

   Wherever the laser strikes the drum the charge is reversed.

   The drum then rolls over more strongly negatively-charged paper.

   Positively charged toner is attracted to negative charges on the drum.

   Laser light is reflected from original paper onto drum.

G The toner is then fused to the paper fibres by means of heated rollers.

Look on
the CD
for more
exam
practice
questions

Did you know?

- The voltage for a spark (between two objects in the atmosphere at sea level) is about one million volts for each metre the objects are apart.

5 Fusion

Have you ever wondered?

Were two scientists, who claimed they could make a nuclear power station in a test tube, crazy?

Key facts

- Two small nuclei can join together (fuse) to release energy.
- The process is called **fusion**.
- Fusion, at present, requires a high temperature.
- The high temperature makes the nuclei move at high speed.
- This high speed allows the nuclei to overcome the normal repulsion.
- The temperature inside the Sun and stars is enough to keep fusion going.

Definitions

- **fusion** The reaction when the nuclei of light atoms, like hydrogen, join together to make the nucleus of a heavier atom.

❶ Examiner's tips

- Fusion shows that strange things can happen at the atomic level.
- Fusion of nuclei could have been predicted as soon as Einstein proposed his theory of relativity in 1905. At that time, however, people did not even know that atoms contained a nucleus!

Can you answer these questions?

1. Which of these apply to fission, which to fusion and which to both?

clean products	release energy without burning	particles join together
chain reaction	happens in stars	products are radioactive
needs very high temperature	produce more neutrons	nuclei split

2. If the loss in mass during fusion of two nuclei is 2×10^{-27} kg, and light travels at 3×10^8 m/s, how much energy is released?

Look on the CD for more exam practice questions

Did you know?

- The materials needed for fusion are readily available in the ocean and the products are much 'cleaner' than fission products.

⑥ $E = mc^2$ and other theories

Have you ever wondered?

What does $E = mc^2$ really mean?

Key facts

- You can hear Einstein's voice explaining this **theory** at:
  http://www.aip.org/history/einstein/voice1.htm
- The products of fission or fusion are less massive than the reactants. This loss in mass is the m in the equation.
- The equation shows that mass and energy are different forms of the same thing.
- The concept of 'conservation of energy' has had to be replaced by 'conservation of mass–energy'.

Definitions

- **theory** Idea that has not been proved by experiment.

Look on the CD for more exam practice questions

❗ Examiner's tips

- The Universe is remarkably symmetrical. So, if mass can be changed into energy, energy can be changed into mass. For example, remember the Big Bang.
- Be aware that scientists have always tried to guarantee credit for their discoveries.

Can you answer these questions?

1. (a) How could Einstein pass information to fellow scientists?
   (b) Might there have been any differences with the ways available to Becquerel?
   (c) What about Pons and Fleischman?
2. Why was the action of Pons and Fleischman not the normal procedure?
3. Why do you think Pons and Fleischman might have rushed to make their 'discovery' public?

Did you know?

- Was it as simple as:

$E = ma^2$ ✗ $E = mb^2$ ✗ $E = mc^2$ ✓

Equations, units and symbols

The following equations will be given to you when you need them.

P2.9 As fast as you can!

$$\text{average velocity} = \frac{\text{displacement}}{\text{time}}$$

$$v = \frac{s}{t}$$

$$\text{acceleration} = \frac{\text{change in velocity}}{\text{time}}$$

$$a = \frac{v - u}{t}$$

force = mass × acceleration $F = ma$

momentum = mass × velocity

P2.10 Roller coasters and relativity

potential energy transferred = mass × acceleration of free fall × change in height

$$PE = m \times g \times h$$

$$\text{kinetic energy} = \frac{1}{2} \times \text{mass} \times (\text{velocity})^2$$

$$KE = \frac{1}{2}mv^2$$

electrical energy = voltage × current × time $E = V \times I \times t$

power = work done ÷ time taken $P = W \div t$

work done = force × distance moved in the direction of the force $W = F \times s$

P2.12 Power of the atom

$E = mc^2$

Units

You should know and be able to use these units.

volts (V)	millivolt (mV)
amps (A)	milliamp (mA)
ohms (Ω)	second (s)
watts (W)	metre (m)
kilowatt (kW)	kilogram (kg)
joules (J)	newton (N)
kilowatt hour (kWh)	becquerels (Bq) (counts per second)
metre/second (m/s or ms^{-1})	metre/second/second (m/s^2 or ms^{-2})
newton/kilogram (N/kg or Nkg^{-1})	kg m/s (or Ns)

Glossary

B2.1 Inside living cells

adenine A base found in DNA and RNA.

aerobic A process using oxygen. Aerobic respiration is respiration that needs oxygen.

amino acid One of about 20 different small molecules that link together in long chains to form proteins. Often called the building blocks of proteins.

anaerobic A process that does not use oxygen. Anaerobic respiration is respiration that does not need oxygen.

aseptic Conditions that are free from contamination by unwanted microorganisms. Aseptic precautions are taken to avoid contamination by unwanted microorganisms in a fermenter.

bases Chemical groups making up part of DNA and RNA molecules. The order of the bases in DNA forms the genetic code.

capillary Very small blood vessel with walls one cell thick. The site of exchange of materials between the blood and cells.

cholesterol A fatty deposit that can build up and block arteries.

coding The strand of DNA that carries the genetic code.

cramp Muscle pain caused by build-up of lactic acid when a muscle is overworked.

cultivated The growth of organisms, such as plants and microorganisms, in controlled conditions.

cytosine A base found in DNA and RNA.

diet Eating a wide variety of different foods to gain all the nutrients we need.

diffusion The movement of molecules from a region where they are at a high concentration to a region where they are at a low concentration.

DNA The chemical that makes up genes (**d**eoxyribo**n**ucleic **a**cid).

double helix The shape of the DNA molecule, like a twisted ladder.

fermentation Using microorganisms to break down nutrients into useful products.

glucose A simple sugar that is broken down in cells to release energy. It is also produced during photosynthesis.

guanine A base found in DNA and RNA.

insulin A protein hormone that controls the level of glucose in the blood and is made in the pancreas.

lactic acid The waste product of anaerobic respiration in muscle cells.

microorganism A very small organism that can only be seen through a microscope.

organelle A part of a cell with a specific function, such as the nucleus.

polypeptide A long chain of amino acids. A protein is made of one or more polypeptides folded into a particular shape.

protein A chemical made of chains of amino acids. Proteins form part of the cell's framework (structural proteins) or carry out a particular job (functional proteins).

respiration The chemical reaction occurring in all living cells. Glucose is broken down into carbon dioxide and water to release energy.

ribosome A tiny organelle in the cytoplasm of a cell where proteins are made.

RNA A chemical similar to DNA that is involved in protein synthesis.

strand One side of the DNA double helix. The two strands are joined by links between pairs of bases.

thymine A base found in DNA.

triplet A group of three bases in DNA that codes for the placing of an amino acid in a protein during protein synthesis.

B2.2 Divide and develop

cancer cell A cell that divides uncontrollably due to faulty genes.

cell division The process through which one cell splits into two daughter cells.

chromosomes Long DNA molecules in the nucleus that carry genetic information.

continuous variable A variable that shows a gradual variation in data across a population.

differentiation In cells, the process whereby new cells develop special characteristics to allow them to do their job.

diploid A cell that contains the full set of 46 chromosomes.

elongation The increase in length of plant cells when they absorb water during growth.

embryo The collection of cells that grows from a fertilised egg in an animal.

foetus The name for an embryo after the eighth week of development in the womb.

gametes Sex cells, such as sperm, ova and pollen.

genes Sequences of DNA inside chromosomes that control the characteristics of an organism.

genetic modification Changing the genetic characteristics of an organism by manipulating genes and introducing them into its DNA.

growth A permanent increase in the size or mass of an organism.

haploid A cell that contains 23 (half) the full number of chromosomes. Produced by meiosis.

hormones Chemicals produced by a living organism that regulate growth, metabolism, and other important processes.

inheritance A term used to describe the passing of genes from parents to offspring.

meiosis A type of cell division that produces sex cells with half the full number of chromosomes.

mitosis A type of cell division that produces cells for growth, repair or the replacement of older cells.

nucleus (pl nuclei) In biology the part of both plant and animal cells that contain its genetic material (chromosomes and DNA). It directs and controls the activities of the cell.

nutrient One of the chemicals needed by an organism to grow.

ovum (pl ova) An egg cell, found in females.

regeneration The special ability of some organisms to regrow parts of their bodies.

selective breeding Breeding plants or animals from individuals that have the characteristics you most want.

species A group of living things sharing the same characteristics which breed together to produce young.

sperm A male sex cell.

stem cell A cell that has the ability to become any type of cell in an organism.

termination Deliberately ending a pregnancy.

B2.3 Energy flow

active transport Movement of molecules into the cell using energy from respiration. It allows the cell to build up a high concentration of the molecules inside the cell.

animal cell Cell containing a cytoplasm, nucleus and cell membrane. Found in animals.

biosphere A self-contained structure that holds all the plants and animals needed for a sustainable environment.

carbon cycle The use and recycling of carbon through respiration and photosynthesis.

cellulose cell wall Rigid outer wall of a plant cell. It gives the cell strength.

chlorophyll Protein in a plant cell that captures energy from sunlight. Found in chloroplasts.

combustion Burning of things like fossil fuels (coal, oil and gas). It adds carbon dioxide to the atmosphere.

crop rotation Changing the crop grown in fields on regular basis.

cytoplasm Jelly-like part of plant and animal cells.

decomposer Microorganisms that digest and break down the bodies of dead plants and animals.

deforestation When large areas of trees are cut down for wood or to create space for humans.

denitrifying bacteria Bacteria in the ground that break down nitrates and convert them into nitrogen gas. Usually found in waterlogged soil.

diffusion The movement of molecules from a region where they are at a high concentration to a region where they are at a low concentration.

disease An illness caused by an infectious organism.

fertiliser Substance added to soil that contains nutrients for plant growth.

food production Farming or fishing to produce food for humans.

global warming The increase in the Earth's temperature that is caused by increasing amounts of greenhouse gases, such as carbon dioxide, in the atmosphere.

glucose A simple sugar that is broken down in cells to release energy. It is also produced during photosynthesis.

membrane Thin and flexible covering of a cell.

microorganism A very small organism that can only be seen through a microscope.

mineral salt Nitrate and phosphate salts required by plants for healthy growth.

nitrates Chemicals used as fertilisers to make crops grow better.

nitrifying bacteria Bacteria found in soil that convert ammonia into nitrate salts.

nitrogen cycle The use and recycling of nitrogen through plants and animals.

nitrogen fixing bacteria Bacteria that live in the roots of some plants (peas, beans and clover). They directly convert nitrogen gas into nitrates.

nucleus In biology, the part of both plant and animal cells that contains its genetic material (chromosomes and DNA). It directs and controls the activities of the cell.

photosynthesis Process carried out in the green parts of plants. Carbon dioxide and water are joined to form glucose. This uses energy from sunlight.

plant cell The building block of plants. Contains a cell wall, cell membrane, cytoplasm, nucleus and a vacuole. Green parts of the plant also contain chloroplasts.

predator An animal that kills and eats other living animals for survival.

respiration The chemical reaction occurring in all living cells. Glucose is broken down into carbon dioxide and water to release energy.

root Part of the plant that anchors it to the ground and absorbs water and mineral salts.

vacuole Sac-like structure in plant cells that controls the amount of water in the cell.

B2.4 Interdependence

adaptation Changing to suit the environment better.

aquatic Living in water.

biodiversity A measure of the variety of species of plants and animals.

competition The battle between different types of organism over the same resource.

conservation Keeping a habitat the same as environmental conditions change.

coppicing Cutting trees and shrubs to ground level to encourage rapid new growth.

environment A particular set of conditions, including water, temperature, light and air.

environmental factors The living and non-living factors which affect organisms.

extreme environment Conditions that are far outside the boundaries in which humans can live comfortably.

global temperature Average temperatures measured across the whole surface of the planet.

interdependence The mutual dependence of one organism with another.

nitrate Chemicals used as fertilisers to make crops grow better.

organism Living creatures such as animals, plants or insects.

ozone A gas found in the upper atmosphere.

phosphates Chemicals that act as fertilisers which are also found in sewage.

pollution Contamination of the environment.

population A group of individuals of a single species living in the same habitat.

predation Killing and eating other animals for food.

recycling Reusing materials instead of additional original resources.

reforestation Planting trees to increase the number of trees.

replacement planting Replacing a tree or shrub by planting another of the same species.

resource Material or energy used by living things.

sewage Solid waste from humans and other animals.

skin cancer A tumour of the skin, usually caused by too much ultraviolet radiation.

terrestrial Living on land.

waste disposal Getting rid of things we no longer need.

C2.5 Synthesis

addition In polymer chemistry, a large molecule formed from alkene molecules added together to form chains.

alkane A hydrocarbon in which all the bonds between the carbon atoms are single bonds.

alkene A hydrocarbon in which two or more carbon atoms are joined by double bonds.

condensation A type of reaction in which two molecules join together to make a larger one, with water as a by-product.

covalent bond A type of chemical bond in which a pair of electrons is shared between two atoms.

cracking A type of chemical reaction in which large alkane molecules are decomposed to form smaller alkanes and alkenes.

double bond Two covalent bonds between two atoms, involving two shared pairs of electrons.

empirical Worked out from an experiment. An empirical formula is worked out by dividing the mass of each substance in a compound by its relative atomic mass.

expected yield The maximum calculated amount of product that can be obtained from a particular quantity of reactants. Also called theoretical yield.

formula (pl formulae) An abbreviation for a substance with two or more atoms. The formula contains the symbols for the different elements in the substance, with numbers to show if there are two or more atoms of a particular substance present.

hydrogenate To add hydrogen to a molecule by a chemical reaction.

monomer A small molecule that can be joined to many other small molecules to form a much larger molecule.

monounsaturated A substance (usually a fat) that only has one double bond.

percentage yield The percentage of a theoretical yield that you actually get in a reaction.

polymer Large molecule made by linking together many small molecules (monomers).

polyunsaturated A substance (usually a fat) that has more than one double bond.

relative atomic mass The mass of an atom compared to one twelfth of the mass of a carbon atom, which has a relative atomic mass of 12. Abbreviated to A_r.

relative formula mass The mass of a molecule relative to the mass of one twelfth of a carbon atom. Abbreviated to M_r.

saturated hydrocarbon A compound of hydrogen and carbon in which there are only single bonds.

sustainable development Meeting the needs of the existing population without damaging the ability of future generations to meet their own needs.

synthesis Making a substance using chemical reactions.

theoretical yield The maximum calculated amount of product that can be obtained from a particular quantity of reactants. Also called expected yield.

thermoplastic A polymer that softens or melts when heated and becomes hard again when cooled.

thermosetting A polymer that cannot be melted or remoulded again once formed.

toxicity How toxic or poisonous a substance is. Very toxic substances have a high toxicity.

unsaturated hydrocarbon A compound of hydrogen and carbon in which there is one or more double bond.

unsaturated monomer A small molecule that can form a polymer because it contains a double bond.

C2.6 In your element

alloy A mixture of metals or metals and non-metals.

atomic number The number of protons (positively charged particles) in the nucleus of an atom.

binary salt A compound of a metal and a non-metal.

conductivity A property of a substance that describes its ability to allow energy (electricity or heat) to pass through it.

electrode A rod of conductive material used in electrolysis.

electrolysis The breakdown of an ionic compound into simpler substances using electricity.

electron A negatively charged particle that surrounds the nucleus in an atom.

electronic configuration The arrangement of electrons in shells around the nucleus.

formulae Abbreviations for substances with two or more atoms. The formula contains the symbols for the different elements in the substance, with numbers to show if there are two or more atoms of a particular element present.

ion An atom or group of atoms with an electrical charge (positive or negative).

ionic bond Force between oppositely charged ions.

isotopes Atoms of an element with the same number of protons and electrons but different numbers of neutrons.

malleable Can be bent or hammered into shape without breaking.

mass number The total number of protons and neutrons in the nucleus of an atom. Also called nucleon number.

neutron Electrically neutral particle found in the nucleus of most atoms.

nucleus In chemistry, the positively charged centre of an atom.

periodic table A chart in which all the elements are put in order of increasing atomic number, with elements that have similar chemical properties arranged in groups.

proton A positively charged particle found in the nucleus of all atoms.

relative atomic mass The mass of an atom compared to the mass of one twelfth of a carbon atom, which has a relative atomic mass of 12.

C2.7 Chemical structures

buckminster fullerene A form of carbon in which graphite-like sheets of carbon atoms form balls or tubes.

carbon nanotube A type of Buckminster fullerene in which the sheet structures of carbon atoms are rolled into very thin tubes. Also called buckytubes.

conductivity A property of a substance that describes its ability to allow energy (electricity or heat) to pass through it.

covalent bond A chemical bond that forms when two atoms share a pair of electrons.

diamond A very hard, natural form of carbon which has a 3-D giant covalent structure in which every atom is joined to four neighbours.

giant covalent structure A structure built from billions of atoms in which every atom is joined to its neighbours by strong covalent bonds.

graphite A very soft, natural form of carbon which has a sheet-like giant covalent structure in which every

atom is joined to just three neighbours.

halogen Family of reactive non-metals (Group 7 of the periodic table).

homeopathic A form of 'alternative' medicine based on 'like cures like' principle using very dilute forms of natural materials.

inter-molecular force The force of attraction between molecules.

simple molecular structure Atoms joined together by covalent bonds to form individual molecules which may be as small as two atoms.

C2.8 How fast? How furious?

catalyst A substance that speeds up a chemical reaction without being used up.

collision theory The theory of chemical reactions that describes how particles must collide with enough energy to react.

concentration The amount of a substance in a given volume of solution.

dynamic equilibrium The equilibrium point in a reversible reaction where the rates of the forward and backward reactions are the same, so the proportions of different substances remain constant.

endothermic reaction A reaction that takes in heat energy from the surroundings.

enzyme A biological catalyst.

equilibrium A balance point.

exothermic reaction A reaction that gives out heat energy to the surroundings.

fertiliser Something which provides the essential minerals that plants need to grow.

Haber process The industrial process used to convert hydrogen and nitrogen into ammonia.

organic To do with living processes.

pressure The force exerted per unit area (e.g. N/m²).

rate of reaction The speed at which a chemical reaction progresses.

reversible A chemical reaction that can be made to work in either direction.

surface area The surface of a solid that is available for chemical reactions.

temperature A scale for measuring how 'hot' or 'cold' something is, usually measured in degrees Celsius (°C).

P2.9 As fast as you can!

acceleration A measure of how quickly the velocity of an object is changing (measured in metres per second per second (m/s²)).

action In physics, one of a pair of forces. The reaction force acts in the opposite direction.

collision When two or more objects come into contact with each other.

gradient A measurement of the steepness of the slope of a graph. The steeper the graph, the higher the gradient.

magnitude A measure of how big something is.

momentum A quantity describing the movement of an object. Calculated by multiplying the mass by the velocity.

reaction In physics, one of a pair of forces. This acts in the opposite direction to the action force.

resistance In physics, a force that acts in the opposite direction of motion. Friction is an example of a resistance force.

resultant force The total force that results from two or more forces acting on a single object. It is found by adding the forces together, taking into account their direction.

speed A measure of the distance an object travels in a given time. Usually measured in metres per second (m/s).

stopping distance The distance a car travels between when the driver sees something and when the car stops. Found by adding thinking distance and braking distance.

terminal velocity A constant, maximum velocity reached by falling objects. This happens when the weight downwards is equal to the air resistance upwards.

vector A quantity that has a size and direction. Force and velocity are examples of vectors. Speed, mass and volume are *not* vectors.

velocity The speed of an object in a particular direction. Usually measured in metres per second (m/s).

weight The force pulling an object downwards. It depends on the mass of the object and the strength of gravity.

P2.10 Roller coasters and relativity

acceleration A measure of how quickly the velocity of an object is changing (measured in metres per second per second (m/s²)).

conservation of energy A law that states that energy can be converted from one form to another but cannot be created or destroyed.

constant speed The movement of an object that covers the same distance every second, neither accelerating nor decelerating.

current The flow of electricity around a circuit, measured in amps (A) or milliamps (mA).

distance A measure of how far apart objects or places are, measured in metres (m).

electrical energy The energy made available by a current. Measured in joules (J).

energy transfer The change in energy from one form to another.

force An action on an object that makes it accelerate, decelerate or change shape, measured in newtons (N).

gravitational potential energy The energy involved in moving anything against the force of gravity, such as lifting an object. It depends upon the mass of the object, the distance moved and the gravitational field strength. Measured in joules (J).

kinetic energy The energy of a moving object, measured in joules (J). It depends upon the mass of the object and the velocity at which it is travelling.

mass The amount of matter in an object, measured in kilograms (kg).

potential energy The energy stored in an object. Measured in joules (J).

power A measure of how quickly energy is transferred, measured in watts (W) or kilowatts (kW).

resultant force The total force that results from two or more forces acting on a single object. It is found by adding the forces together, taking into account their direction.

speed A measure of the distance an object travels in a given time. Usually measured in metres per second (m/s).

theory of relativity A theory put forward by Albert Einstein that connects different areas of physics including mass, energy, gravity, movement, space and time.

velocity The speed of an object in a particular direction. Usually measured in metres per second (m/s).

voltage The difference in electrical energy between two points that causes a current, measured in volts (V). It is sometimes called the potential difference.

work done The energy transferred by a force on a moving object, measured in joules (J).

P2.11 Putting radiation to use

activity The number of emissions of radiation from a sample in a given time. Sometimes this is given as counts per minute (cpm) or, more correctly, as Becquerels (Bq).

alpha particle The largest form of particle that can be emitted as radiation from unstable nuclei. It is equivalent to a helium-4 nucleus.

atom Smallest particle of any given element. Atoms are themselves made up of electrons, neutrons and protons (so-called subatomic particles).

atomic (proton) number The number of protons present in the nucleus of all atoms of one particular element.

background radiation Radiation that is all around us all the time from a number of sources.

beta particle Particle form of radiation that can be emitted from the nucleus of radioactive atoms when they decay. It is equivalent to an electron.

electron Negatively charged particle that forms part of every atom. Electrons orbit the positively charged nucleus.

gamma ray An electromagnetic (EM) wave emitted from the nucleus of some radioactive atoms.

half-life A measure of how quickly some radioactive substances decay. It is the average time for half of the atoms originally present to have decayed.

ionising radiation Form of radiation that causes ionisation in atoms through which it passes – the atoms lose electrons from their outer shells and so become charged overall – they become ions.

isotope Atoms of an element with the same number of protons and electrons but different numbers of neutrons.

magnetic field Region where moving charged particles experience a force.

mass (nucleon) number The combined total number of neutrons and protons in the nucleus of one particular isotope of an element. Also called nucleon number.

mutation Change that takes place in a living organism, often as a result of interaction with radiation.

neutron Neutral-charge particle that is found in the nucleus of all atoms, except hydrogen.

nucleus (pl nuclei) The central, positively charged, part of all atoms.

proton Positively charged particle that is found in the nucleus of all atoms.

radioactive dating Method of determining the approximate age of a material or substance.

radioactivity The random emission of radiation from the nuclei of unstable atoms. The process of emission changes the type of atom.

radon gas Naturally occurring, radioactive gas that is emitted from rocks underground.

random process Process such as radioactive decay in which the timing of the next event cannot be predicted.

sterilisation Process where bacteria and viruses on an object are destroyed. Sterilisation can be carried out using radioactive sources.

X-rays Electromagnetic (EM) waves emitted by metals when they are bombarded with electrons.

P2.12 Power of the atom

attraction Describes a force that pulls two objects together.

chain reaction The sequence of reactions produced when a nuclear fission reaction triggers one or more new fissions.

daughter products The two nuclei produced when a nucleus undergoes fission.

decay series A sequence of radioactive isotopes and their radiation. When a radioactive isotope decays, it may form a new radioactive nucleus. This in turn decays into another nucleus. The series goes on until it reaches a stable nucleus.

electric current The movement of charge – electrons in a wire.

electrostatics Effects created by electrical charges that do not move.

fission The reaction when the nucleus of a heavy atom splits into two smaller nuclei.

fusion The reaction when the nuclei of light atoms, like hydrogen, join together to make the nucleus of a heavier atom.

insulation A piece of material that does not conduct electricity. It stops charge from flowing.

neutron A particle found in the nucleus of most atoms. It has no charge.

nucleus (pl nuclei) The central, positively charged, part of all atoms.

nuclear reactor The part of a nuclear power station that holds the fuel rods and control rods. It is where controlled fission takes place to produce heat for generating electricity.

radioactive Describes a substance that gives out ionising radiations like alpha, beta and gamma.

repulsion A force that pushes two objects apart.

thermal energy Energy associated with a hot body. Measured in joules (J).

theory Idea that has not been proved by experiment.

Answers

B2.1 Inside living cells

1 DNA (page 9)

1. The four bases in the DNA molecule are adenine, thymine, cytosine and guanine.
2. The bases line up in the DNA molecule in pairs: adenine with thymine, and cytosine with guanine.
3. A triplet codes for DNA because each set of three bases codes for a particular amino acid. The triplet decides where one amino acid is placed in the protein chain.
4. Enzymes are proteins. They are made from chains of amino acids. The order of these is controlled by the sequence of the bases in DNA.

2 Fermentation and microorganisms (page 11)

1. A culture medium is a liquid containing all the nutrients and a source of energy that microorganisms need to multiply.
2. Fermentation is a process where microorganisms use up the nutrients in the culture medium and produce waste products and other substances.
3. A section of human DNA coding for insulin is cut out and then inserted into bacteria. The bacteria now contain the DNA for insulin and make it.
4. The advantages of using microorganisms for food production are: that they reproduce at a very fast rate, they are easy to keep in a fermenter, they can be grown anywhere and they can be fed on waste products from other industries.

3 Proteins (page 12)

1. RNA is different from DNA because it has a base called uracil instead of thymine, and is a single strand, not a double strand like DNA.
2. The genetic code is carried by DNA as the sequence of bases.
3. Each triplet of bases codes for an amino acid. The sequence of triplets controls the order of the amino acids in the protein chain.
4. There are two type of RNA, messenger RNA and transfer RNA.

4 Respiration (page 13)

1. Respiration is needed to release energy from glucose.
2. Aerobic respiration takes place when cells have plenty of oxygen; anaerobic respiration takes place when cells are short of oxygen.
3. glucose + oxygen → carbon dioxide + water (+ energy)
4. Diffusion is the movement of molecules from an area of high concentration of those molecules to an area of low concentration.
5. Cramp is caused by a build-up of lactic acid in the bloodstream.

5 Exercise (page 14)

1. Your heart rate increases during vigorous exercise to increase blood flow to carry more oxygen and glucose to muscle cells, and to remove carbon dioxide from the cells.
2. The graph shows an increase in breathing rate from 12 to 16 breaths per minute in the first five minutes. The rate stays at 16 for 10 minutes and then slows down to 12 again. The graph changes because the rate of breathing increases with exercise and then returns to normal when the exercise ends.
3. Increased breathing results in increased energy because it provides more oxygen to increase the rate of respiration in the cells.
4. An alcohol thermometer can only measure to about 0.1 °C at best. A digital thermometer is more precise and can measure to 0.001 °C.

6 Diet and exercise (page 15)

1. A study found a link between the amount of cholesterol people ate and heart disease, so people believed that more cholesterol in the diet increased the risk of heart disease.
2. Some diets may mean that you do not get sufficient of some food types, or too much of others. This can have medical effects.
3. A healthy lifestyle means eating the right amounts of each food type and getting regular exercise.
4. Regular exercise in important to keep muscles strong, and to exercise the heart so that it is able to cope with extra demands placed on it.

B2.2 Divide and develop

1 Cell division (page 17)

1. During mitosis each cell makes an identical copy of its chromosomes before it divides. When the cell splits each daughter cell contains an identical set of chromosomes to the original cell.
2. Cell division is needed for growth, repair and the replacement of older cells.
3. Meiosis produces gametes by cell division. Each pair of chromosomes in the original cell is split, one chromosome from each pair going into each of the new cells. This means that the chromosomes in gametes have half the number that a normal body cell has, and each cell has a different set of chromosomes.
4. The difference between mitosis and meiosis is that mitosis produces identical, diploid cells with identical chromosomes; meiosis produces haploid cells with different sets of chromosomes.

2 Growth (page 18)

1. Growth is a permanent increase in the size or mass of an organism.
2. Dividing cells undergo differentiation so that they develop the special characteristics they need to do their job.
3. Plant growth is affected by factors including light intensity, temperature and the availability of nutrients in the soil.
4. Every human starts life as a single fertilised cell. It grows to become a foetus, and will increase in mass about 3000 times. After the first year, growth is steady until puberty when there is a growth spurt and the individual will grow to their full size.

3 Stem cells, tough decisions (page 19)

1. A cancer cell is dangerous because it has no Hayflick limit. It will keep dividing to form a tumour.
2. A stem cell has no Hayflick limit because it is undifferentiated and can keep dividing to form any type of body cell.
3. Some stem cells come from embryos and there are people who think that it is unethical to use embryos for stem cell research.
4. A 36 week old foetus is viable because its nervous and breathing systems are developed enough for the foetus to survive outside the womb, but those of a 16 week old foetus are not.
5. Athletes taking steroids can suffer side-effects including liver failure, facial hair growth and deepening of the voice in women, and impotence and breast development in men.

4 Plant growth (page 19)

1. Plants need the right conditions of light, water, nutrients, temperature, carbon dioxide and water in order to grow.
2. Some plants are adapted to grow in low light conditions. This may mean that they are small and grow slowly compare with plants that are adapted to needing more light. Plants that need high levels of light may not produce enough glucose to allow them to grow properly in low light levels.
3. Auxin concentrates on the shaded side of shoots, making the cells elongate more so the shoot grows towards light.
4. Hormones produced by the developing embryo inside the seed cause the ovary to develop into a fruit.

5 Artificial selection and cloning (page 20)

1. Regeneration is the ability to regrow body parts.
2. Use a bull and cow that have the desired characteristics and breed from them. Select the calves that have the desired characteristics, and when they are adult, breed from them. Repeating this over many generations increases the chances that more offspring will have the desired characteristics.
3. The nucleus is removed from an egg cell and replaced with the nucleus of a body cell. These are fused together and stimulated to divide and grow into an embryo.
4. Cloning can result in animals and plants that have useful characteristics that they would not normally possess. People are mainly concerned about human cloning, and feel that it is unethical to clone copies of humans.

6 Gene therapy (page 21)

1. Human genetic diseases are caused by faulty genes. These are passed from one generation to the next and cannot be cured.
2. Viruses are used in gene therapy to carry replacement genes into cells to replace the faulty genes.
3. Once a gene is introduced into reproductive cells, it will be passed on to future generations. Not enough is known about the long-term effects of gene therapy.
4. Gene therapy can be used to stop disease being passed on to future generations because the faulty gene is replaced by one that works properly, so the faulty gene will not be passed on.

B2.3 Energy flow

1 Cells in close up (page 23)

1. Roots are transparent. They do not contain chlorophyll. They cannot photosynthesise because they are below the ground.
2. Respiration occurs all the time.
3. The reactions are exactly the same, but in reverse.
4. Glucose is used for growth, respiration and other cell processes. Most oxygen is released to the atmosphere, but some is used in respiration.

2 Remarkable roots (page 24)

1. Nitrates are needed to build proteins for the growth and repair of cells.
2. Nitrates are absorbed from the soil by active transport and are carried through the plant by the xylem vessel along with water.
3. Glucose is needed for respiration to facilitate active transport.

3 Controlling carbon (page 26)

1. Carbon dioxide is thought to contribute to the greenhouse effect where heat is reflected back onto the Earth's surface instead of being released to space.
2. Rainforests are being destroyed as a result of the need for wood, grazing land for cattle, and building land for industry and homes.
3. Fewer rainforests will lead to less carbon dioxide being removed from the atmosphere, so there will be an increase in carbon dioxide concentration and therefore an increase in global warming.
4. Microorganisms help with the decay of plant and animal matter and so help to put nitrates back into the soil. They respire, which causes an increase in the carbon dioxide levels in the atmosphere.

4 Natural nitrogen (page 27)

1. Excess use of nitrate fertilisers can lead to eutrophication. The nitrates leach into rivers and streams and build up, which causes an increase in the algae and bacteria in the water. The algae stop light passing through so photosynthesis cannot go on under the water. As a result, the water is deoxygenated and plants and animals die.
2. Farmers can leave fields fallow (no planting) or plant leguminous vegetables to restore nitrate levels.
3. Nitrogen can be converted to nitrates in the soil by decomposers changing proteins to ammonia and nitrifying bacteria changing ammonia to nitrates, or by nitrifying bacteria on the nodules of leguminous plants.

4. Denitrification is the changing of nitrates to nitrogen. It usually occurs in waterlogged soil.

5 Production panic (page 28)

1. Limiting factors are light, temperature, water and carbon dioxide concentration.
2. Plant growth slows during darkness because no photosynthesis can occur. 24-hour daylight would increase plant growth.
3. Proteins are needed for any plant growth. Many parts of the plant need protein.

6 Population problems (page 29)

1. Sustainable development is carrying out life today without compromising future generations.
2. Organically grown crops are not genetically modified, have no pesticides used in their production, can only be produced in soil which is classed as natural (no chemicals used). Only natural fertilisers can be used.
3. Intensive farming produces a high yield and the crop can therefore be sold at a lower price, but many chemicals are used in the process and natural environments and biodiversity may be threatened.
4. Finding the correct plant/bacteria/animal balance would be very difficult because many of these organisms produce varying amount of oxygen and carbon dioxide in different conditions.

B2.4 Interdependence

1 Amazing adaptations (page 30)

1. Large paws to give a large surface area for walking on ice, white coat to camouflage itself from its prey, thick fur for insulation.
2. Gills to take in oxygen, scales to help to waterproof, shape is streamlined and the stripes help to camouflage from potential predators.
3. Rabbits compete for food, space and mates.
4. Coloured flowers are required for attracting insects for pollination. The more colourful, the more insects will visit.

2 Extreme environments (page 32)

1. Life in the deep ocean is dark. A sense of smell is needed as sight is limited. Conditions vary from 300 °C in hydrothermal vents to 1–5 °C in deep ocean.
2. Desert environments have cacti which have no leaves, only spines, to reduce water loss and very deep root systems to enable maximum water uptake. Polar bears live in Arctic and have thick fur for insulation, small ears to reduce heat loss to the environment, and white fur to enable them to camouflage themselves from prey.

3 Challenging competition (page 33)

1. Increase in the numbers of cases of skin cancer in humans, rise in temperatures globally, causing same effects as global warming.
2. Eutrophication, eventually leading to death of underwater plants and animals.
3. Pollution in the city causes buildings to become covered with dark soot, therefore the dark coloured peppered moth is more camouflaged and less likely to be seen by predatory birds.

4 Plastic pollutants (page 34)

1. People are not educated to think recycling is important. Packaging in Britain produces huge amounts of waste products. People are not inspired by the government to recycle.
2. Toxic gas is given off when plastics are burned. Plastic does not rot naturally in the environment. Plastics takes up large amounts of space in landfill sites.
3. Carbon dioxide and methane are both greenhouse gases which contribute to global warming.

5 Deciphering data (page 35)

1. 300 ppm.
2. Largest source is the burning of coal. Causes acid rain which damages forests, lakes and buildings.
3. 2 °C.
4. As carbon dioxide levels increase, global temperatures increase.

6 Compulsory conservation (page 36)

1. Biodiversity is important for the survival of all species in food chains. If one species is destroyed, this can have a knock on effect on many other species.
2. Coppicing, reforestation and replacement planting are conservation techniques.
3. Succession involves natural selection in the environment, conservation is the maintenance of current species.
4. The World Conservation Union keeps track of all endangered species and seeks to maintain and increase the current populations.

C2.5 Synthesis

1 Cracking and reforming (page 37)

1. Simple distillation does not separate mixtures of miscible liquids.
2. Reforming joins together small molecules.
3. Alkanes only have simple covalent bonds, alkenes have a double bond between two carbon atoms in their molecules.
4. C_4H_{10}
5.

2 Saturated and unsaturated (page 39)

1. It may be joined with other identical molecules to make a polymer.
2. No, because it does not have any double bonds, so cannot join to other molecules.
3. (a) poly(styrene)   (b) poly(phenylethene).

3 Types of polymers (page 40)

1. Thermoplastics melt on heating, thermosetting plastics do not.
2. Unplasticised/polyvinylchloride.
3. Examples are nylon, lycra or terylene.

4 It's all fat, but does it make you fat? (page 41)

1. Monounsaturates only have one double bond, polyunsaturates have more than one double bond.
2. Margarine.
3. There are stronger forces between molecules in saturated compounds than in polyunsaturated ones.

5 Making new chemicals (page 42)

1. (a) 18 (b) 27

6 Using chemical reactions (page 43)

1. Na = 23, Cl = 35.5, Ca = 40, K = 39, Br = 80.
2. NaCl = 58.5, KCl = 74.5, CaBr$_2$ = 200, NaBr = 103, KBr = 119.
3. 7.3 g.
4. 200 tonnes.

C2.6 In your element

1 The properties of metals (page 44)

1. Crystals of the metal from which the lamppost is made.
2. Aluminium, nickel and cobalt.
3. Aluminium, copper, magnesium and manganese.

2 Atoms of elements (page 45)

1. In the nucleus.
2. The elements contain different numbers of protons (and electrons and neutrons).
3. A sodium atom contains 11 protons, 11 electrons and 12 neutrons.

3 Electron arrangements (page 46)

1. 19.
2. The number of outer electrons = the group number (except for group 0).
3. Na = 2, 8, 1, Mg = 2, 8, 2, C = 2, 4, Ar = 2, 8, 8.

4 Ions and ionic bonding (page 48)

1. K^+, Br^-, O^{2-}, S^{2-}, Li^+, I^-, Mg^{2+}.
2. Its ions are not free to move, so it cannot conduct.
3. Ca^{2+}, Rb^+, e^-, e^-.

5 Electrolysis (page 49)

1. Lead bromide is insoluble in water. It will only conduct when molten and the ions become free to move.
2. (a) chlorine   (b) copper.
3. (a) $2e^-$ (b) cathode.

6 Isotopes and relative atomic mass (page 50)

1.

	hydrogen 1	hydrogen 2	hydrogen 3
protons	1	1	1
neutrons	0	1	2
electrons	1	1	1

2. The two atoms are both carbon atoms. Carbon-12 contains 6 protons, 6 electrons and 6 neutrons.
   Carbon-14 contains 6 protons, 6 electrons, and 8 neutrons.
3. 44.4.

C2.7 Chemical structure

1 Covalent bonding (page 51)

1. The electrons involved are shared by two atoms.
2. any of the following: hydrogen, oxygen, carbon dioxide, nitrogen, chlorine (and many others).
3. (a) six (b) two
4. NaCl

2 Simple structures (page 52)

1. (b)
2. zero
3. (a) The atoms stay covalently bonded.
   (b) The molecules separate from each other.
4. Small covalent compounds evaporate easily/have a low boiling point. They need to be a gas so that we can smell them.

3 Giant molecular structures (page 53)

1. Covalent bonding
2. The strong bonds between the silicon and oxygen atoms have to be broken throughout the structure before it can melt. This takes a lot of energy.
3. All the outer electrons are in fixed bonds. There are none to spare to move about as an electrical current.
4. You need to break the strong 3-D covalent bonds in order to cut through it.

4 Giant metallic structures (page 54)

1. The outermost electrons can move through the lattice.
2. (a) can be hammered into shape
   (b) can be drawn into a wire
   (c) can conduct heat energy
3. (b)
4. Impurities make the gold harder so it will not wear away as quickly.

5 Carbon structures (page 55)

1. Giant (covalent) molecular structure.
2. Layers of carbon atoms are rubbed off onto the paper.
3. All the atoms are held in a rigid structure by string bonds.
4. Three.

6 Models and medicine (page 56)

1. first they use simulations on a computer
   then they are tested on tissue cultures in a lab
   then they are tested on animals
   then they are tested on healthy volunteers
   then they are tested on a small number of volunteer patients
2. They are not tested before being used on a patient.
3. There is no reliable experimental evidence that homeopathic medicines work.
4. When a treatment or medicine works because the patient expects that it will work.

C2.8 How fast? How furious?

1 Making and breaking bonds (page 57)

1. Outside.
2. Bonds are strong forces that hold atoms together into molecules. To break the bond you have to use energy to overcome the forces.
3. Heat energy (accept a spark/flame).

2 Concentration and surface area (page 59)

1. (a) longer time, slower reaction
   (b) longer time, slower reaction
2. C
3. Increase the pressure
4. They must collide with enough energy to break the bonds.

3 Temperature and catalysts (page 60)

1. They increase the speed.
2. The number of particles with enough energy to react increases.
3. The mass of the catalyst is the same at the end as at the start.
4. The speed halves so that the reaction takes twice as long.

4 Reaching a balance (page 61)

1. The right-hand side.
2. It speeds up the reaction but does not alter the equilibrium position.
3. The yield increases.
4. The yield decreases.

5 Practically speaking (page 62)

1. Any two from the following.
   Any remote place, such as the tip of an aircraft wing.
   Any dangerous place.
   During a fast reaction.
   To take readings over a long time period.
2. On the data-logger or on a computer as graphs and/or tables (spreadsheets).
3. Liquefying the ammonia reduces the number of product gas molecules in the system and so moves the equilibrium point to the right (to produce more ammonia).

6 Fertilisers: artificial or organic? (page 63)

1.

Artificial fertilisers	Organic fertilisers
easily absorbed	preserve biodiversity
work faster	may improve soil structure
produce bigger harvest	are slow release

2. Nitrogen, potassium and phosphorus.
3. The range of organisms present in the environment.

P2.9 As fast as you can!

1 Speed and velocity (page 64)

1. Metres per second or m/s.
2. Velocity is speed in a particular direction, but speed does not have a particular direction.
3. $240 \div 4 = 60$ m/s.
4. (a) Average velocity = $100 \div 50 = 2$ m/s (from one goal to the other).
   (b) Average speed = $250 \div 50 = 5$ m/s.

2 Acceleration (page 65)

1. Metres per second each second or m/s^2.
2. Its size (magnitude) can change, and so can its direction.
3. (a) Acceleration = $(70 - 0) \div 350 = 0.2$ m/s^2.
   (b) So that passengers can still move about in the train safely.
4. (a) Your sketch should show a line sloping downwards.
   (b) Acceleration = $(7000 - 8000) \div 200 = -5$ m/s^2 (decelerating).

3 Force, mass and acceleration (page 66)

1. Your weight acts downwards and resistance from the chair acts upwards.
2. Your sketch should show driving force (forwards), drag (backwards), weight (downwards) and resistance from the ground (upwards).
3. (a) Force = $300\,000 \times 3 = 900\,000$ N.
   (b) Resistance = $1\,000\,000 - 900\,000 = 100\,000$ N (backwards).

4 Falling (page 67)

1. Constant velocity does not change. Speed and direction stay the same and there is no acceleration.
2. If an object is not accelerating, the resultant force is zero.
3. (a) Resultant force on Sharon = $600 - 200 = 400$ N (downwards).
   (b) Sharon's velocity will increase, but her acceleration will decrease.
4. The astronauts would go on accelerating as they fell. Without air resistance there can be no terminal velocity so they would just fall faster and faster. (Also, without any air resistance, their parachutes would not work.)

5 Stopping safely (page 68)

1. Factors that increase stopping distance are: high speed, driver's slow reactions, wet road, worn tyres, faulty brakes, etc.
2. The car cannot begin to slow before the driver uses the brakes. The longer it takes the driver to react, the further the car goes before the brakes are used.
3. Momentum = $1500 \times 40 = 60\,000$ kg m/s
4. The light bulbs are less likely to be damaged if the packet is dropped. The bubble wrap should absorb the momentum gradually so that there would be less force on the bulbs.

6 How dangerous? (page 69)

1. The risk of injury or damage when crashing in a simulator is 0%.
2. Taking risks can be thrilling and people choose to go skiing. So they are willing to accept the risk.
3. Risk of getting wet feet = $(2 \div 10) \times 100 = 20\%$.
4. The experienced worker has a better understanding of the risks and may know the right thing to do in a dangerous situation.

P2.10 Roller coasters and relativity

1 Work, work, work (page 70)

1. The unit for work is the joule (J).
2. The distance moved must be measured in the same direction as the force.
3. Work done = $25 \times 150 = 3750$ J (or 3.75 kJ).
4. Work done lifting one packet = $10 \times 1.5 = 15$ J.
   For 30 packets, the total energy transferred = $30 \times 15 = 450$ J (or 0.45 kJ).

2 Power and electrical energy (page 71)

1. A watt is the unit for power. It is a rate of energy transfer of 1 joule per second
2. Power = $300\,000 \div 4 = 75\,000$ W (or 75 kW).
3. Energy = $230 \times 1.8 \times 8 = 3312$ J (or 3.312 kJ).
4. Energy = (electrical power) × time in seconds
   = $150 \times 1800 = 270\,000$ J (or 270 kJ).

3 Potential energy and kinetic energy (page 72)

1. The unit for *KE* is the joule (J).
2. $GPE = 0.1 \times 9.8 \times 15 = 14.7$ J
3. KE of ball = $\frac{1}{2} \times 0.056 \times 50 \times 50 = 70$ J
4. (a) KE of bus = $\frac{1}{2} \times 10\,000 \times 12 \times 12 = 720\,000$ J (or 0.72 MJ)
   (b) KE of motorbike = $\frac{1}{2} \times 400 \times 60 \times 60 = 720\,000$ J (or 0.72 MJ)
   They have the same kinetic energy. Although the bus has more mass, the motorbike is going faster.

4 How roller coasters keep moving (page 73)

1. For example, kinetic, gravitational potential, electrical.
2. $GPE \rightarrow KE \rightarrow$ thermal (and some sound).
3. Electrical energy is transferred to kinetic energy. The motor causes a force on the car which makes it accelerate as its velocity changes.
4. The passengers experience forces and changes in acceleration that are thrilling. They enjoy taking a risk in a safe environment.

5 Going round in circles (page 74)

1. The speed is stays the same, but the direction of the velocity is changing.
2. Your diagram should show a horizontal resultant force towards the centre. (You could also show Wendy's weight and the reaction from the chair.)
3. The satellite accelerates because its velocity is changing all the time.
4. Your diagram should show George's weight as a force towards the centre of the circle.

6 Einstein and relativity (page 75)

1. Checking a hypothesis by thinking about the implications.
2. Einstein's theory was not accepted at first because there was no experimental evidence.
3. The theory is accepted now because there is experimental evidence such as nuclear energy and relativistic effects.
4. Without repeatable experimental results, scientists are unwilling to accept a new theory.

P2.11 Putting radiation to use

1 Radioactivity: what and where from? (page 76)

1. gamma   2. alpha   3. gamma

4.

name of radiation	symbol of ray	type of charge	penetrating power	ionising power
alpha	α	positive	low	high
beta	β	negative	medium	medium
gamma	γ	none	high	low

2 Structure of an atom (page 78)

1. $^{6}_{3}\text{Li}$

2. (a) $^{2}_{1}\text{X}$ + $^{2}_{1}\text{X}$ + $^{4}_{2}\text{Y}$

(b) 1   (c) 2.   (d) 4.

3. $^{3}_{1}\text{Z}$ $^{2}_{1}\text{Z}$

3 Radioactivity in action (page 79)

1. helium (alpha particles are helium nuclei)
2. (a) Alpha particles would not pass through the cardboard.
   (b) Roughly the same number would pass through with and without the powder.
   (c) If the level of the powder falls, the reading on the detector will rise.

4 Changes in activity with time (page 80)

1. About 125 Bq.
2. Just over 1400 years.
3. 2000 years.

5 Background radiation (page 81)

1. (a) cosmic rays
   (b) radiations from medicine and the nuclear industry
2. Charged particles from space trapped in the magnetic field of the Earth.

6 Dangers and risks (page 82)

1. There is a long list which should include:
   keeping sources locked away when not in use, not pointing them at anyone, only picking them up with tweezers or other long range tools, no eating or drinking when they are in use, no one under 16 year old to use.
2. Any *three* of, for example, mutation of DNA, sterilisation, radiation sickness, death.
3. Any *three* of, for example, applications in medicine, tracing movement of liquids e.g. oil leaking from underground pipes, dating historical objects, industrial, for example, thickness control.
4. Your discussion should include arguments in favour such as saving lives in case of fire and against such as the fact that they use radioactive materials of quite long half-life.

P2.12 Power of the atom

1 Fission and chain reactions (page 83)

1. (a)

Key	
●	U-235 nucleus
◉	Daughter product
○	Neutron

(b) A neutron strikes a U-235 nucleus.
This nucleus splits into two daughters and three neutrons.
One of these neutrons strikes another U-235 nucleus
This also splits as before, producing three neutrons.
Two of these neutrons cause further fission.
None of the six neutrons produced cause further fission.

2. Each falling domino causes the next to fall. In a chain reaction, something happening causes the same thing to happen elsewhere.

3. 256 neutrons will be freed after the following, 2, 4, 8, 16, 32, 64, 128, 256, eight stages.

2 Power stations (page 85)

1. (a) The reaction will die away.
   (b) The rate of reaction will increase rapidly.
2. Lowering the rods will slow down the reaction as more neutrons will be absorbed and not cause further fission.

3.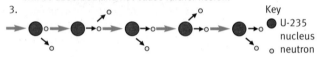

3 Electrostatics (page 85)

1. They will both be attracted and try to move closer.
2. Electrons are in orbit around the nucleus which contains the protons. The protons are held tightly in the nucleus.
3. The negative electrons are held by the attraction from the positive nucleus.

4 Uses and dangers of electrostatics (page 86)

1. The frame is made positive so that it will attract the negatively charged paint drops and so save paint. There will be less paint wasted.
2. The rotating drum is charged positively.
   B Laser light is reflected from original paper onto drum.
   C Wherever the laser strikes the drum the charge is reversed.
   D Positively charged toner is attracted to negative charges on the drum.
   E The drum then rolls over more strongly negatively-charged paper.
   F This stronger charge pulls toner to the paper.
   The toner is then fused to the paper fibres by means of heated rollers.

5 Fusion (page 87)

1. Fission: nuclei split, produce more neutrons, chain reaction, products are radioactive
   Fusion: particles join together, needs very high temperature, happens in stars, clean products
   Both: release energy without burning
2. $E = mc^2 = 2 \times 10^{-27} \times 3 \times 10^8 \times 3 \times 10^8$ $E = 1.8 \times 10^{-10}$ J

6 $E = mc^2$ and other theories (page 88)

1. (a) Telephone and telegraphy by wire were well established and radiotelegraphy was just being tested. These would be in addition to the low tech methods of letters, books, etc.
   (b) Becquerel could not have used radio.
   (c) Pons and Fleischman could have used the internet and most other modern ways.
2. Pons and Fleischman did not circulate their discovery to other scientists by publishing them in scientific journals. This would have allowed independent verification as other scientists would have tried to reproduce the discovery.
3. Pons and Fleischman might have thought that another group was close to beating them to the discovery. It seems that they were mistaken rather than making a fraudulent claim as has happened on a few other occasions.